THE RETURN
OF
THE HERETIC
The First Seven Years

Discourses with
MASTER TEACHER

ENDEAVOR ACADEMY
Certum Est Quia Impossibile Est

©2011 Endeavor Academy
The Return of The Heretic: *The First Seven Years*
Discourses with Master Teacher

International Standard Book Number (ISBN-10): 1-890648-14-0
(ISBN-13): 978-1-890648-14-5

Library of Congress Control Number: 2011922361

Published By:
Endeavor Academy
501 East Adams Street, Wisconsin Dells, WI 53965, USA
Phone: +1 608-253-1447
www.themasterteacher.tv
Email: publishing@endeavoracademy.com

Contents

Ye have heard that it hath been said,
An eye for an eye, and a tooth for a tooth:
But I say unto you, That ye resist not evil:
but whosoever shall smite thee on thy right
cheek, turn to him the other also.
And if any man will sue thee at the law,
and take away thy coat,
let him have thy cloak also.
And whosoever shall compel thee to go a mile,
go with him twain.

A Sip From
The Holy Grail

Where is the dilemma of fracturedism or duality? In lack of what is termed, in a religious sense, "Love." No one on this planet practices love — hear this — because if you did you wouldn't be here. Your definition, in duality, of what love is, is not true. To you, love is finding security, to fend off the inevitable death that you at this perception think is real, and refuse to look at. Love can be nothing else but that to you — finally. Bottom line! Love, finally, — taking out the ideas you have about it in regard to moonlight, "graspation," copulation, whatever else you think occurs in love — is only communication. Love is finally only communication. I want to say this again, and I said it before, it is finally only my ability to communicate to you who I am. Do you see?

If we share Romeo and Juliet symphony that is playing now in totalness, you and I are totally in love. How could we help but be? We are energizing and feeling the same responses spiritually that occur in us as we recognize that we are one thing! That we are finally only one thing! Do you see? That's what love is. Does it have to do with coupling? Not really. You could walk into the United Nations tomorrow and if everybody could suddenly communicate with each other all war would cease, everybody would immediately give of themselves and become whole. Of course!

Your inability to love, or communicate, is because of your inability to see who you are. You think you have to protect something. You walk around trying to protect it. You think that there is an element in you that has to defend itself. What do you defend yourself against? Huh? Why are you afraid? Huh? What are you afraid of? What is it? Why are you fearful? You can't love because you are fearful. You can't love because you don't know that I am you.

The difference in you and me right now is I can extend to you and know that you are me; and I love you totally and absolutely, I assure you. The only manner in which I can do that is by knowing that you are me. And I must love myself first before I can love you. It won't work any other way. If I have a residual of doubt in me — through a non-awakening or because I haven't become whole — that somehow I am not okay, it is impossible for me not to project that onto you. It can't be done. Do you see? That is why we teach that all judgment is self-judgment. What else could it be but that? Who else could you judge but yourself? If you judge yourself falsely, you will automatically judge everything outside yourself falsely. Of course! Instead of extending the truth of you, from you, you will project it from you in your isolation. You see? If you look at me now and say, "There is some sort of a weird guy standing up there with a dirty shirt on and no socks, and he is waving his arms around. I wonder who he is", what have you done? You have identified yourself, have projected out from yourself; and everything that you have accumulated in your brain (which is a facsimile about this level of consciousness), you are trying to correlate to determine who I really am.

So, what do we do? We start with the premise — and you start with this premise right now and put everything else aside — either everything I am saying to you now is absolutely true or there is no truth in it. Now what are you going to do? Now can you judge? Haha, I got you! Now your mind is going, "Oh, that can't be. Some of the things he says might be okay, but then some of the things I think that he might say might not be okay, because some of the things he says are Spinoza and some of them are Neo-Platoism and some of them are probably Kant and some of them are Jesus Christ or Buddha or Dr. Fu Manchu..." or whoever the hell else you think is influencing your thinking. That's absurd! All you're doing is, you are just categorizing in your mind at this level what you think is true. Since you don't know who you are, you can't possibly judge anything here. It's absolutely impossible.

If you have an opinion about something it's wrong! Because the earth is wrong. There's no truth here (impossible!); no justice here (impossible!), unless you will allow it to be, unless you allow it to be true; unless you allow it to be just, through your own purity, through your own innocence, through your coming to know who you are; through your establishment of your invulnerability in your power, to your surrender to your translation or transformation. There's no other way. Is that religious? I don't know. I told you earlier, religion today on earth is a science, not a *ré*ligion, not a returning, not a *re*collection, not a coming back to who you are.

You are evolving. You can see that you are evolving, therefore you must evolve to something. If there is something, you must have been there originally. If you can conceive of it, it must be true. Astounding! It's an astounding idea. You have it now in your mind. When you go out of here today, remember you have chosen to be what you are. Okay? There is no outside force that is making you the way you are. It's impossible! Do you have it? Yes, but how do you facilitate it?

Questioner: Have I chosen not to know what I am?

Well, why would you do that?

Q: I don't know...

No, you don't believe me. No, you don't believe that you have a choice. So now you have identified yourself as *self* and told me you have chosen not to know. No, if you knew, you would know automatically because it is transformative.

Q: But when you say '*you*' are you not referring to me as a personality, or are you referring to me as God?

Do you know me and love me absolutely as being you?

Q: No.

Okay, well then, get that. When you do, then you'll know. Remember, it's still your idea. You are now expressing an idea from some state of judgment that you have made. It's not true. It's very difficult, because every time you express yourself you are only coming from where you are.

I say to you absolutely — and I want you to hear this; this is the most important thing you'll ever hear — there is no such thing as individual personalities. Ha, you hide on this earth because you think you're different from me. You're not! Do you have a boil on your rear? Huh? You hide something. "I am not going to let you know that something is wrong." There are no secrets here! What is it you would keep secret — that you are lustful, that you are dirty, that you... (bleeech!) and all that junk? That isn't true. We share a totally common heritage of truth. You are on earth because you are hiding.

Those of you who think that you're on a spiritual path (to the extent that you strive to do good and that), let me say this to you: You are actually hiding. You are afraid of the truth. Because the truth will make you whole. And if you become whole, it will be unto all things, and you will lose your individuality. Listen to me: when you totally come to know that you are God you will still be just as you are now.

Remember, there is only one consciousness. You have an idea that in your transformative process, you are not going to know who you are; or that the death process (because you equate it with no-thing) will stop your identity. It won't. It won't. You can't leave consciousness. You can't die. This is very fundamental to everything that we teach. You are here solely because you think you are going to die. That's why you're on earth — no other reason. You think you can die; and you can't.

[Background music playing] It's astonishing to me that a reductionist could hear that kind of music and think that that was a bunch of notes that we hear, and that somebody at this level put them together somehow — I don't know how — and it turned out to be something that everybody could communicate and understand; rather than recognizing that contained in every entity is the totalness of perfection that is manifest to the degree that they are able to manifest it. And that includes literature and music and poetry and art and science — whatever you do to extend the truth from you to what it really is.

Is that divine? Of course it's divine. Is this cup divine? What else would it be but divine? This cup is spectacular.

This cup is whole unto itself. This cup is finally what your idea of this cup *is*. If I say to you, in truth and in love and engendered energies, that this is the *Holy Grail*, there, you go, "Oh, that is the Holy Grail!" Now you have changed your mind about this cup. Do you feel that? Oh, you found it — what you have been looking for all of your life. Here it is. One sip of this elixir of life and you can come whole and total.

Is what I just said to you true? Of course. Totally true. Now what have you done? You transformed your *idea* about what this is. You have changed your mind about what you think it is. What is the transformative process but changing your mind about something? Finally you keep changing your mind and changing your mind and letting go and letting go and giving up and going through this spiritual progress until you end up at a single truth. You will come to know what the single truth is by figuring out that you can't know what it is and giving up to the nothing that it is for you at that moment. And that's the truth.

And now we have the dilemma of a fractured earth. We have the dilemma of the reality that appears to be in the body: "This is so; this is true". We have the dilemma of the terrible chaos of war and starvation and defense and anger and remorse and recrimination and all of the other ugly incredible things that you carry around in your mind because of your inability to forgive yourself, and come to know who you are. You share mutual pain with other entities who hope that things are going to work out, that things will come to pass that will be okay here. My dear one, you cannot perfect an illusion. I have said it many times to you, and I say it again: The fault of the earth is the conception of the earth. The fault of the earth is your idea about it. Is there a remedy for duality? How would you, by a process, remedy the conception of duality?

How about the Beatitudes? Let's take Christianity, let's take Jesus Christ: When he stood up and said the things that you do not do, that if you do, you'll find the Kingdom of Heaven, he made a true statement. Out of transpersonal psychology (where we were dealing), let's deal with the fact that you resist evil: He said, "Resist not evil. Blessed are the poor in spirit." You are not poor in spirit. You resist evil. Okay? Of course, that's why you are here; because you do those things.

Now, you will immediately defend yourself in that regard because you think you're *you* and that's where you fail. You see? Do you see that? The admonition to resist not evil means literally "resist not evil." It doesn't mean resist a little bit. What did you do? You judged what was evil and what wasn't. I say to you: Detach completely and defend yourself against nothing. So did Christ. Of course. You go through life trying to prove something to somebody. You go through your life until you find death, attempting to validate yourself: "I must be worth something. I've got a doctor's degree in humptydumptyness (or whatever you have); I am this; I went to school; I did this; I can prove that."

Have you ever watched people walk in the room and everybody presents who they are? They don't know! They have no idea who they are. What a terrible dilemma! Then they go to the secret of their own closet and they are all down inside and saying, "I'm not really that way. I've had to go out and pretend. I wish I could be like them. They think that, they don't..." Nobody does.

There is not a single winner on the planet earth. I positively guarantee you! You go outside yourself and say, "I wish I could be like that." That's absurd! There aren't any winners. What is going to happen to them? They are going to get old and their nose is going to rot off. Huh, what are they are going to do? Their children are going to leave them and they are going to grow up; everything crumbles. There is no reality here!

Do you think that there is a God that would have anything to do with this planet? Come on, come on, you made it up. You don't know who you are. You are going to protect yourself and pretend there is a force outside of you that is causing this to occur to you. There isn't; it's just your idea. We're back to ideas again. You have a false idea of who you are. And that's what the problem is.

Communication: How do I communicate? Have I said one single thing to you that you don't already know? No! Is it possible for me to say anything to you that you don't know? No! You have limited the amount that you think you know. You know everything. I absolutely guarantee you, you know everything.

You've got yourself at this level of consciousness squeezed down; you are blind, deaf and dumb. You are an embryo and you have gone outside yourself and found these other little things and they correlate into self. You know, "Let's take your personality to God." That's absurd! You're not real! No wonder you are in desperate pain. That's painful.

See, what has happened with you, there is a maturation process that has gone on cellularly in your symbiotic relationship, in your body, and suddenly you are looking around and you see that you are different, you are thinking different than other people around you. And you say, "Something must be wrong with me." So why don't you go to another insane "earthy" and he'll give you some medication that maybe can keep you insane! Don't wake up. Well go about half way and say, "I am perfectly willing to accept that there are some divine spirits above us, but after all we must stabilize this insanity." Huh, isn't it strange? Somewhere along the line you qualify yourself.

If you didn't you'd be in Heaven. Do you see? You are choosing this. You are choosing to be self rather than God. Isn't that amazing? Huh?

I stand here as some sort of a light for you, like a beacon, an energy beacon; it's what a Christ is. Christ is what you will be. So there are energies that flow out of me in truth simply because I have arrived at a truth that is the truth. You already know it too, so you look at me and say, "Oh, that's true."

All of you here are avatars. All of you here are standing at the Omega point, looking at this. You are awakening from your dream. You see that this is not true. Try *that*. Try *that*.

Everything that can possibly occur to you, as you remember it, has already occurred. Of course, there is nothing new. There is no idea that you could possibly have that has not happened. Huh? If it weren't then we'd run out of things finally. It would go to an end; time would be linear. There is no linear time. Hm? You were never born and you cannot die. Hello, isn't that spectacular?

"Well, I wouldn't want that to be." Why not? "Well, I don't know." What have you done? You have identified with the body. You think this is real. You think that's real. It's not. It's your idea about it. The energies that you feel in this room, as you meditate, and as you have quiet times, are individually responding in you by definition. Don't look at anyone else. That means nothing. Where are *you* with it? Where are *you* judging it? Where are *you* allowing yourself to come to the truth? Remember that everything I am saying to you is true, or false. If you choose to reject at this moment everything that I am saying to you, let me see you do it. You can only then reject yourself, and you cannot possibly go to nothing — it's impossible.

There is no such thing as *no* thing. Try it. Try to die. Sit there and go, "I am going to die. I am determined I am going to die." And you try and die and, no, you are still here. Think of the most ugly, awful, incredible skulls and... Go ahead, look at death! That's a great process. Let me say this to you: You cannot discover that you are eternal until you look at death.

The process of transformation is a process of going through death to know that you can't die. Did you know that? Huh? That's what it is. It's expressed in exoteric Christianity as "being born again" and all of the other things that go with it. But I assure you that it's true. These entities that you see die, in the consciousness, and then perhaps are resuscitated, have reached a little beyond and come back with the stories of truth. There is more to it than that, but they are in truth.

When you go through your transformative stage you will literally see the light. What do you think seeing the light is? That's a real light, just as they report in the death process. Huh? You don't believe that. That's why you are here. Ha,ha. You don't think you can do that.

That's why we teach: "die." That's why we teach: "look at death." That's why we show you: "please look down the line and see that you are in a nursing home, dying of old age at this moment." And you have shucked that aside; you're pretending that's not true. You are pretending that all the people didn't starve to death out there. You are saying, "There is nothing I can do about that. I'll hang onto myself." And you are going to fail. If you attempt to stay in self, you will fail and you will grow old and you will die, and you'll have pain. I say to you: You don't have to do that. That you will refuse to play the game of death that is played here at this level of consciousness, on this earth, on this planet, and decide to transcend it and that you may do it at this moment. Not only that but you can only do it at this moment.

Come on! There you go. Wow, look at that. This is not a thought process. This is not a process of thought, is it? Because thought requires self-identification. You will fail automatically, if you establish yourself and attempt to cleanse it, or attempt to do it. It won't work! Do you know what happens? You engender a lot of energies up here, then you pull them down and make magic out of them. That's what occurs.

"Do you mean to say that there really is a power right here now?" You can call it God if you want to, or don't call it God. I don't care what you call it. Call it something you don't know anything about that's here because you are conscious. It is just above you and it energizes. And it's right here now and you can reach up and get that. From a religious standpoint it is like saying, "I only see God when I go to church on Sunday" and if God is not here now he is nowhere. If there is a power in the universe it's here. It wouldn't be anywhere else. Where else would it be but here? It's with you all the time.

Is it possible to reach up and come to know that? Sure. That's the process that you are going through in your body now. That's the transformative process that's occurring in you. [Inhales deeply] Oxygen. Real deep.

Don't analyze it. You are in a process of awakening. And boy does that feel good if you really come to know that. Uhahuhahu. There you will be standing alone and the thought will come to you that there really is a power working on you to cause a change to come about in you, and you'll go, "Oh, my goodness sake." I assure you that it's true. I assure you that it's happening to you. I assure you that it is happening despite anything that you do. I assure you that everything that occurs in your life, all apparent pain, apparent sorrow, apparent love, apparent joy, all identification of yourself, lead you to one single truth, okay? That you are in a process of awakening.

I define the earth as a hatchery, okay? Or an embryo stage. A cocoon stage that you are going to evolve to truth on. That's precisely what it is. It has no value unto itself at all. You may stay in the nursery as long as you choose to, or you may leave it at this moment. Are the birth pangs a little painful? I suppose. But you are going to get jerked out into the light whether you want it or not.

It's very joyous. What is it finally an admission of? That you are powerless. That you have nothing to say about what goes on here. Not only that you have nothing to say and are powerless, but that everything is okay and that the more powerless you are the more strength you'll have? Ahaha! Even unto your own surrender in death, at which time you will have total strength? Ahaha! That sounds familiar. This isn't real! You are dreaming. Wake up. Wake up.

Do you want to leave right now? Go ahead. You feel suddenly responsibility. You feel suddenly, "Gee, I created these things and I am responsible for them and maybe I'd better stick around for a little while and maybe I'd better stick around and go through another death or two before I finally come to know that you're responsible for nothing here on earth. Nothing! Nothing! You are free. You have created in your own illusion false responsibility in order to establish your own security, dummy! You've made it up. It's tough. So all the other things that you've made up outside of you are going to attack you if you dare walk around and say, "Hey, be free, be easy, let it go. Be happy, woohoo! You can't hurt me! Whee!" "Everybody is going to come after you." No, they won't. Do you know why? Because you are going to come to truth. Remember this: You are not the judge of your own motivations. So fail. The times of your greatest success, I assure you, have been the times that you thought you failed. You have absolutely nothing to say or equate with a perfect template that sits here that's speaking. You can't arbitrate it, you can't negotiate with it. What do you do with it? Surrender to it!

"Ah, come on, that's weak. I am not going to accept that nonsense."

Blessed are the poor in spirit. Theirs is the Kingdom...

"I don't believe that."

Nobody believes anything that is said by everybody. Everybody who is awake and says the same thing, and that people are awake and don't believe it, and that's why they are not awake. [laughing] Isn't that amazing? I say to you in truth that I recognize that you are me totally in slowness. That you are a part of me that is here that is not awake, and I don't mean to imply hierarchies, because there isn't any such thing. I know positively that you are perfect. Absolutely. Absolutely, positively, there is no part of me that does not accept your perfection. Remember if there were, that would mean that I am not perfect myself or do not believe that I am. And have therefore projected out from myself that insecurity or a corruption to mind. The truth is within you and nowhere else. And you are coming to know that is true.

So are the quantum physicists coming to know finally that, as they experiment, they change the experiments by their thoughts. Astounding, isn't it? They come to know that finally everything is subjective. That's a horrible idea. They appear to look at things and finally they discover that they made the whole thing up themselves.

The entire universe is a single thought. It could be nothing but that. There is either perfect unity in everything

19

that you can conceive or there is perfect chaos. Yes, it would be perfect unto itself if it were possible. There is nothing in between. Some things are not in unity and some things chaotic. That is impossible. If you believe it, it is why you are here, because you are looking at it at a slow speed. You are looking at it in dimness. You are looking at it crunched, with your consciousness not expanded to where you can see the truth.

Be of good cheer, you can't fail. You've been in failure. The expression "Let those that can hear, hear" always comes to mind, because as I look I see where you are with these particular thoughts or energies that I am giving you. The process cannot fail because you cannot fail. Any perception you have of yourself that is not perfect or divine is not real. Find your peace of mind from that. I don't know how you can deal, as your consciousness would begin to expand, with the intense apparent injustice and pain and greed that goes on at this level of consciousness and self-identification. The travail that ensues as your energies awaken can be very intense.

You have a tendency to defend yourself finally, and you say, "I am entitled to something, aren't I?" And do you know what I answer to that? My dear friend, you are entitled to everything. Why do you settle for just something? And you say to me, "I'll be perfectly happy if I can just have a little." And I say to you, no you won't. How can you be happy with something that keeps changing? Every time you think you have it right, pooooff, it's gone. Oh, it's terrible. There is only a single truth and you are it.

Therefore be joyous. Why not? Hmm? Sure. A lot of people get into Eros, "eat, drink and be merry, for tomorrow we die." The problem is tomorrow you don't die. You eat, drink and be merry if you choose, but remember everything is cause and effectual in space/time. You never escape consequences of your acts, which are finally your thoughts. Therefore you never escape consequences of your thoughts. Are you taping this? It just flows.

"But what about it," you are saying. Which literally means there are no idle thoughts and everything that you think, you are responsible for. If that is true and thirty thousand people starved to death last night, you must be responsible for their deaths; and you are, by your conception of their death. Amazing! True. Did they really die? Of course not. That's absurd. There is no death.

Be of good cheer. You would not be here if you had not already won. The path of coming to truth is a path of becoming true. There is no truth here; only becoming truth. And each time you become truer, you exalt more in the realization of your own freedom from the nursery. You put away your toys and you understand that you are a creator. And that as you extend the idea of who you are, you become more Godly. And as you become more Godly you extend more from you and become (what, finally?) Universal Consciousness. Of course. Will you feel differently when you are Universal Consciousness than the way you are now? No. The only difference will be that everything that you say will be truth. And there will be no opinions about it. That's what Heaven is. Or it will be totally false. Because it cannot be in between.

Questioner: If everything you say is true, then why say anything?

Because you don't believe it.

Q: No, I don't mean now.

I didn't. I am not. The moment that you actually believe everything I say is true and know it is so, you won't be here either because I am not here. I am only here by your conception of me. I stand in the middle of your dream.

I have disrupted the fabric of your consciousness and I am saying: Wake up. Wake up. Wake up.

Wake up. It's that simple. Never mind your ideas about it. None of them are true. Period. How could they be? *You* are not true. Does that seem simple? Too simple. You say to me, "If I am not true I might as well die and not be here." I'll say, okay, do that. Then you are getting close. "Well, I don't think I'll die yet. Instead of that, I better go home and pay the milk bill." Ahaha! Isn't that funny?

Finally, all fourth level consciousness is an equivocation. It's the in-between stage of maturation, starting with very slow speed, mineral, moving through vegetable consciousness, conscious of consciousness, on up through animal, finally on up to this level, and on further. Okay?

We'll have a little quiet time. I guess everybody is getting very quiet. There is a lot of energy in here.

Minds are going to open up and you'll hear and you'll see differently. Then you are not blind any longer. You hatch. You look around and you have little wings coming out. It's true. It's fine. Then you realize that all the junk that you handled down in here, all the pain that you felt, and all the hate and defensiveness and hanging on and clinging and being in hell, meant absolutely nothing. It wasn't real! And here is a big band of angels reaching down to earth, "Welcome, weary traveler, come home!" It's that easy. It's *that* easy.

Everywhere you go at this stage you are being watched. And each time you turn towards that light a little bit, it'll [claps]. "Yes, here comes another one." They prune. They go through the garden and they prune out the people waking up. Sometimes you get all tangled up with weeds down here and you converse with them. That doesn't make any difference. You are going to blossom. Sometimes you begin to blossom and you look around, and everybody around you is still in a bulb, in a cocoon, and they are asleep and you go "What's the matter with me. I don't feel like I am a bulb or in that... Can't these people see? Are they asleep?" They are asleep. And you're waking up. But you only wake up alone for yourself. That gets kind of lonely sometimes. That's okay. There are those of us who share in your awakening. That's why we're here. Here is heaven. Here is the beautiful field of flowers. Down here they are still as seeds. See, they have all the potential in them. Hm? They aren't awake yet! Don't be that. Don't be in the nursery now.

You are all graduated. I guarantee you, you graduated. I wish you could see this. I have you all graduated. Whoop, there you are, this is my class. Okay? This is the class of 26-47-49-52-78-1. This is the eternal class. This is the only class that there is. I assure you that what I said is very true. I share but a moment with you, the joy of our recognized separation, so that we may come to union together, in truth. That's all I do. I know just a *fraction* of a moment ahead of you that I am you, that you are me. And you go, "You're right!" Zoom!

What did we do? Made a universe. What did we do, coming together? Like a zygote. Boomo! A whole universe, a whole new constellation. A whole new cellular drive. All the new consciousnesses in unity spreading out. By what? That simple recognition that you are me. Total extension. Total surrender. Total acknowledgment. Total truth. And the incredible discovery that that's all there ever was, was that moment. And all of you are feeling it now. And each time you feel it is the only time you can ever feel it. But each time you do you are closer. And when you finally come whole completely, you'll say, "I always knew that. How could I have forgotten?" And it won't matter, because you'll know that it took everything that has occurred in space/ time to allow you to maturate, to allow you to become whole. So instead of looking back on it and saying, "I could have done it before," you'll say, "Thank you." Because then you'll know the truth of you. And you'll see that the other you was never real. Astonishing. And it's happening to you right now.

I'll be back with you in a little bit.

Keep your hands up and there is the Lord of Hosts and the sun is shining and there, that's it. Don't die to find it. Die to self to find it. There are billions of earths waiting for you. The whole universe abounds in consciousness. Wake up.

Wake up! Here's a batch! Wake up! Here batch, here! Feel that? It's all just consciousness, it just waits for you to ask. Here I am. Oh. Lost in the stars. Wake up! Good tidings. Great joy! Can't lose! No death! How easy will your mantle be when you come to know that truth. How joyously will you walk the earth. What a great teacher you will become, when the truth becomes known unto you! You cannot fail. There is no failure. If there were, I would have told you so. What would you fail to do? So be ye perfect. Never mind anything else. Feel within you that power of truth, and all else is laid aside. Keep good countenance. Be prudent. Carry the truth in you. You have nothing to prove. We already know who you are. We already know who you are, Angel.

Those of you who want to hang around forever, can. Those of you who want to journey forth onto this path that you tread may do so. You walk a path of truth.

Q: No matter how you struggle and strive.

Ah, and you can't walk out this door alive. It's very simple. It's incredibly simple. Simple! Easy! Be joyous and loving. Give everything away, don't hold onto anything. Don't hold on. Don't hold on. Don't hold on. Let go of everything. Then you can love. Imagine the freedom of letting go of everything and loving. It's incredible. There is nothing like it.

Are you going to come? Woooh, it's late!

*An evil and adulterous generation
seeketh after a sign;
and there shall no sign be given to it,
but the sign of the prophet Jonas:
For as Jonas was three days
and three nights in the whale's belly;
so shall the Son of man be three days
and three nights in the heart of the earth.
The men of Nineveh shall rise in judgment
with this generation, and shall condemn it:
because they repented at the preaching of Jonas;
and, behold, a greater than Jonas is here.*

Sown In Thorns
And Raised In Lilies

We are going to look at, in just a moment, the incredible idea of the reality of the resurrection, as you come to your truth, as is lived for the first time the reality of you in your maturity, in your coming into your new sense of consciousness.

If you really stop to think about it, of what significance would the resurrection, or ostensibly the resurrection, the overcoming of death of the carpenter two thousand years ago in Nazareth, have possibly to do with you? Yet in reality, if it doesn't finally have to do with you, it has nothing to do with anything. Was it of historic significance, that a man who had, through manifestations of particular qualities in miracle ideas, or the performance of miracles, which led subsequently to the idea that he was a savior, or an advanced prophet — there was nothing new about that. Nothing.

The idea of the crucifixion certainly wasn't new. That was one of the common methods of execution in its day, wasn't it? Previous to then the road to Jerusalem was strewn with over eight hundred people who had been hung on a cross. Historically, it apparently didn't mean anything; at least for a considerable length of time it was barely mentioned, in what was termed the civilized world. Yet in your memory patterns, as you sit here tonight, are constituted all of the remembering that occurred in the drama that was played out in the incredible allegory of you going through a process of limitation into a process of remembrance of your initiation of whence you came, and that's what's enacted on Easter Sunday morning.

Does it have to do with you? It has directly to do with you. Some time it would be interesting to talk about layers of awareness in the Easter story — wouldn't it? — as esoterically presented, the idea that the crucifixion and resurrection occur in your microcosm, or in your body. These are all high truths. Nothing has ever occurred in what we would call the realm of space/time consciousness that did not have directly to do with you as you are at this moment, as you think of yourself. And, in fact, it has nothing at all to do with anything, except it directly pertains to your state of consciousness in attempts to identify the sense of beingness that you find yourself in at this moment. The true value of everything that has ever occurred, historically, in what is defined as history, or cause and effect, or relationships in fracturedism, have finally only to do with you now, at this moment, in regard to how it is re-cognized in your individual system of identity

Was it you, then, who were taken before Pontius Pilate and condemned to death, hung on a cross? Of course. Was it you, then, who mocked in the streets at the time of the crucifixion? Of course. Was it you that stood guard and rolled dice for the cloth? Of course. Was it you who fell asleep in the Garden of Gethsemane, at the time of the trial of the passion of man consciousness overcoming his limitation, and going through the process of death in order that the recognition of the eternity of consciousness in the universe could be manifest? Of course it was you that felt so.

The identity Jesus, as constructed author of *A Course In Miracles*, speaks very plainly of his identity of you at this moment; the relationship of man-consciousness in regard to Jesus. Of course. Are we saying then, that the salvation or the Atonement or the enlightenment, in the manifestation of evil that is evident at this stage of consciousness, can only be discovered or uncovered by you individually, awakening to the truth of you? The answer is yes. It will not be accomplished in any other way.

The directive for you, by all awakened identifications, is only, "Follow me. You may do as I have done." It could not be any other way. The hesitancy on your part, as identified in your limited state of consciousness, to fully pursue the idea of eternity is difficult because it requires finally the absolute acknowledgment of the unreality of you as you have defined yourself in all of space/time. We'll be back in just a moment.

As I sit here with you, I have a perfect recollection of what occurs in the death process, of what happens when you die. I could give you very explicit details in regard to examination of the feelings of the occurrence of the death and awakening process. The incredible sudden realization that there is no turning back at the time you enter the portal. The sudden determination to see it through at that point and retain identification of it, in the total abandonment of the process. The peace that passeth understanding, the ordeal is over and you come into the truth of recognition that you are still here, still alive. The glory of the light that you behold and truth that comes about in you.

Are these things that you have read about or heard about or had some dimension or inclination to accept or deny? Of course not. I am here to proclaim to you that the awakening process that you are going through, the resurrection, the Atonement, occurs in you totally, in the transfiguration of the cellular construction that you identify at this moment in space/time as body and in no other fashion. Period.

There are no such things as half truths. There is no such thing as a partial Atonement, as a partial state of forgiveness, a partial state of non-guilt, a partial state of innocence, a partial state of defenselessness, a partial idea of abandonment. The whole dilemma that you have ever experienced in identification of selfness has always been the idea that there were variant forms of truth or unity or love or reality. There aren't. Light is light and dark is dark. The transformation of your consciousness is a singular event that must occur in you, individually, as you recognize yourself at this moment and in no other fashion.

All of the teachings that have been given and expressed to man in his corruption have been to direct you to the realization that, as you are now at this moment constituted in consciousness, you are literally all that there is in that sense of beingness, I assure you. If you would choose to identify me, in your limited state of sleepiness or death, as an elder brother at this moment, you may well afford to do so, but if you give me qualities in which you can therefore identify your own duality you will be in sin, you will be in death, you will be in limited identity. Okay? The absolute truth, finally, that all conceptions are invalid is the highest sense that I could attempt to convey to you, although obviously it's not understandable. What we are saying actually is that not only is everything that you see about you unreal, but your idea about it at the highest level is also unreal. You are finally, at the highest level, not even a conception of yourself. You simply are a state of beingness, in truth and union and love and bliss and happiness and joy.

Has it occurred to you that as I sit, then, as your elder and say these things to you why you simply don't turn and rush into the arms of truth? Has it occurred to you that if what we teach or what Jesus expresses in *A Course In Miracles* is true, that you simply don't want to remember it? You, individually, not the constructs of your semi-consciousness outside of you. They have no relationship with the truth, except as you have identified them. Just you. Just you do it. Does that then require a form of courage, of determination, of full endeavor, of commitment? I guess. As long as you don't attempt to measure what degree you are committed to.

I may say to you in absolute truth, the idea of persecution is nutty, it's insane; there is no possibility, if there is a God, that you could be persecuted. I heard someone last night on television say that God was inflicting this form of pain in order that you would somehow overcome it and come to some recognition. That's a strange sort of a god. There is no truth in that. That somehow He allows an evil force to stand against Him in some manner by whatever devious methods he might be allowed by the strange idea that limited consciousness has about truth. There isn't any truth in that, there never could be. The only thing, as we have said many times before, that could ever be evil or cause you pain or death or distress, is yourself. And yourself in defiance of your Creator, which is more difficult.

Is it you, then, who were persecuted and abandoned? Killed? And raised up and was born? And reconstituted consciousness in body in a limited manner with full cognition of death? Of course it was you. And that process is what you are going through right now.

Jesus, in *A Course In Miracles*, says, and I won't be quoting: I gave you a rather graphic demonstration of the idea that there is no death. And the energy influx at that time, space/time, which was just a few days ago, really, in reality, has been with you ever since. It came in the formulation of Pentecost and is now contained in your genetic memory. It is impossible, as you are here at this moment, not to remember the occurrence of two thousand years ago, because you are constituted only in memory. That's literally all that you are. Your forbears remembered you and conceived you, and made you in the image of themselves in limitation and thus it has ever been, since the occurrence of the schism. You are Adam's dream. You are your own dream. The effects that appear outside of you, you have constructed.

"Are you saying to me then that the man Jesus made up — okay? — within his limited framework of consciousness the crucifixion and resurrection?" Of course he did. Of course. Is that a little tough for you? He says in *A Course In Miracles*, "I wasn't real, as I was identified and as I identified myself I was not real."

There is a move afloat in regard to propitiation that somehow God came down or descended into man and that Jesus knew very well that he was fulfilling the law. Uhuh. Sure. You remember, man becomes God in remembrance of his Godhood. And while he is man he is very man, and no one can go through the portal of death and retain identification of it but you, individually, and death is not your idea of death, as subtracted from you and observed in limited consciousness. Death is literally the process of annihilation of you as you are constructed. That's what being born again is; dying to be born again

So what do we celebrate at Easter time? We celebrate the overcoming of death, or the recognition of the specie as identified man on the planet earth being in fact a god. "Know ye not that ye are gods?" "Greater things will you do than I have done." What are you waiting for? The determination of the identification in limitation to hold onto selfness and *literally* construct murder and greed and hate and anger have nothing at all to do with you, brother. You have a single assignment here, and that's to come to your own individual Atonement, and none other. That is your sole function in consciousness. And that's what you are coming to know.

Are miracles possible? Is it possible for the resurrection to be physical and real and for him to have come back in a body? Of course. That's the least that you can do. If it is in fact your illusion, and I assure you it is, and it is your dream, why can't you change it? Do you prefer the idea that there is something outside of you that can attack you and cause you to be sick and die and feel pain? Isn't it easier for you, brother, to come at least intellectually to the idea that you're causing all this? You go from there. Then transformatively it'll come about in you; you will be able to see the truth, won't you? Of course.

The energies that you are feeling now in this transformative process are very real and they are very genuine. And they *are* occurring in you. It *is* your resurrection, isn't it? What does Jesus say in *A Course In Miracles?* "I changed my mind about it. And if one mind is changed, all minds are changed." There is no such thing as separateness. You cannot be separate from God. You are an extension of Him in truth, literally. The idea that you can be separate, or that you made yourself, and that you could construct outside of you visions or apparitions or ideas that would subsequently die with you, is simply a sign of your fractured thinking. It has absolutely no reality at all. The world is literally not real and was not here at all until you remembered it, and will not be here when you discover it's untrue through the discovery of who you really are.

Teach that, brother, that's the truth. Have I then given you an assignment, a responsibility? Of course, of the highest nature, to the recognition of you in the extension of your love, to overcome, so that the world can be saved. There *is* only one Son of God. There is only one state of consciousness, as manifest by the extension of unity in the universe, and that is your state of being in your consciousness. There is nothing but that.

Did you then die on the cross and were you in fact in the tomb for three days and did you rise again? Of course. Shall I do an analogy in your body of what occurs glandularly during that process, so that I can bring you into this moment rather than have you remain historic in identification of it? What's the difference? You are all memory anyway. This is the time when you do it. This is the time when you remember, when the ancient melody plays for you. This is the time when the incredible joy of the recognition of your eternity flashes across your mind. And you will at that moment pay no longer any direct heed to anything that occurs on earth. You will simply subtract it; you will see the unreality of it.

It's a momentous occasion that is applauded in Heaven, as each of you individually comes into that truth. We await your homecoming. Everybody else is home. Just you linger. All of the things that you have constructed outside of you in your projections in order to retain this false identity, Lucifer, are not real. There is only one Son of God and it is you, prodigal. What are you waiting for? Are you waiting for something, something outside of you that is in your memory banks to somehow show you the way? They can, they can. They're just your thoughts, your limited thoughts in consciousness. You have created indeed, but you have created falsely because you are false to yourself.

We teach a course in know thyself, brother. Does that come about through an element of forgiveness? Of course. It is impossible for you to be unjustly treated. There is no such thing as exchange. You literally cannot have anything. You may only be and you may only be truth.

The icons and the symbols and the stories, the parables, all stir deep memories in you in your karma responses. And this is what you want to stimulate, isn't it? You want to come into a focus so that everywhere you look — okay? — you see that identity of union coming together, of singularity fitting into your patterns of truth. And that's what's occurring. Indeed, that's what the spiritual path is. But it's up to you.

He is risen indeed. He *is* risen. As He says in *A Course In Miracles*, the earth is literally not here. It was repaired the moment that the schism occurred. And you actually, in reality, have never left home. No wonder you get these stirrings in you that somehow you don't belong here and you're not here. You're not! That's nice to know. He is risen indeed. *You* have risen indeed. If you are in responses, where you're in your path, where you're in your Bethlehem, where you're in a temple, where you're teaching, where you're in your Gethsemane. Be there. That's okay. You have risen indeed, brother.

"My Lord, why hast Thou forsaken me." You live with that, literally, on a moment by moment basis.

"Father, into Thy hands I commend my spirit." "It is finished." Ffffwwwwwssssst! It's gone.

I am interrupting your dream. You are beginning now to have difficulty locating me. You are beginning, in your own consciousnesses, to extend from you your own identity, through recognition of the light. Wow! What a strange notion that finally you'll never be able to locate yourself. Can you feel this? I have absolutely no idea where I am, because I am not anywhere. It may appear to you, now as you project me, that I am somehow sitting here in a place in space/time and that you will retain identities. I am not. I am not here. Huh, why would I be here? You're not here either. [laughing] The highest truth — Jesus talks about this in the *Course* too — the highest truth I can give you is when you come into true conception, or an idea about yourself, you'll see obviously you could not be located anywhere. Where would you locate yourself outside of truth? You couldn't. Do you know what I am really saying? I *am* you. Consciousness, the state, Dharma, in the universe — all of it is consciousness — only has one manifestation of awareness, or Son, that has been caused by Him to establish causation, and that's you, in your consciousness. There isn't anything else but that.

The single difference that would be apparent to you in that regard is the absolute recognition, as a Son of God, that you did not make yourself. All right? You are not, in that regard, origin, but all of your creations, who you subsequently, through the extension of your truth, foster, are in fact your sons. And since there is finally no difference in Godliness, or Fatherness, you are indeed the Father. That's the circle. Astonishing, isn't it?

Creation, then, which could be identified in some forms as a form of action, never multiplies because it is always full. Jesus in *A Course In Miracles* says, "Consciousness is always maximal." You are always utilizing to its fullest, no matter what you may think about it. And that's a nice thing to know. There are no idle thoughts, so all of these beautiful thoughts that you are having about Easter, are healing in the world. You cause no pain to anyone as you stay within your own love and truth. You are a great healer in that process. You don't accept the idea of death any longer. You see that you can't heal the illusion in separation. And through your own Atonement and coming to truth you look through it and it's made whole by your idea of its wholeness. That's very lovely. That's precisely what occurred in the resurrection.

You are risen. You are risen indeed. Be of good cheer. You offer your brother lilies now, not thorns. As you share that gift of gratitude and love with him, he will extend back to you the truth of you. In that forgiveness are you made whole.

One little idea of total love, carried to its completion, transforms the world forever and has. That's the power of your thoughts, Son of God. You cannot *use* it in limitation, but only in the truth of your extension, because it is literally your creative capacity. And your misuse of it, and your inability to extend it from you, are what cause pain and death. True. You die because of your attempts to hold on in limitation, to grasp and keep separate from the truth, yourself.

Creation and love depend on flow. The Sea of Galilee thrives, it has outlets. The Dead Sea is dead; everything flows in and nothing comes out. All humans on earth as constituted are Dead Seas. They have no outlets. They have no communication processes. They communicate only with themselves and have no reality in truth. Because love is communication. Love is recognition of yourself in love and purity.

So you have been fishing off the wrong side of the boat, haven't you? Ha ha, nice analogy. Yes. Yes. Some of you had some high recognitions and decided to go back to Galilee and fish anyway. We don't talk much about that. Peter? Come to your truths. It's all in you and it's all lovely. You walked that seven miles, huh? You passed your Palm Sunday? You are born in your lower regions; you're coming into your truth. You have passed your heart and compassion center, and you have moved very rapidly up to your prophesying ability. The raising of Lazarus is man's love for man, not Godly. You brought about your crucifixion, and Golgotha in your head, and your enlightenment in your crown. As you come to the glory of your reality. Astonishing, isn't it?

Happy Easter. Thank you, we'll be back.

The notion of man risen from the dead always implies the sign of the cross, or the horizontal man who becomes — what? — upright — all right? — at his point of junction, which is the spot of man-godliness, and moves vertically in order to transcend. There was always given in the beginning the Word, which is not the name of God, which, say, in the Jewish tradition, would be "Jehovah", but rather the sounding of the Word, as in Elohim, which is really a word, a chant, a sounding, that will cause — what? — a verticalness to occur in the dead or the dead to rise.

Neither Thanatos
Nor Eros

G reat stuff, huh? Nice stuff. We teach here in truth that everything is only your perception of it. If you are confused you will cause confusion. I assure you you caused the death of ten thousand people last night because you conceived of death. What you do is refuse to accept responsibility for it and go outside and blame somebody else. Inevitably, you have to blame someone. You say, "I don't know." Somewhere, underneath, you are blaming somebody, because you are not willing to accept the responsibility for yourself, are you? And as soon as you won't accept it for yourself, by nature, you must blame somebody else for it. But you did it, you did it. You cut that grandma's throat last night. Now you are going to go outside yourself, catch your own projection and put it to death because it killed somebody else. Ha, ha, ha. You are allowing your own projections to attack you.

Oh my goodness sake my brother! Thank you. We teach in energy, in light and truth. Let it occur. Come on, we teach communication through identification. I teach in truth that you are me. Oh, brother. One of these days it will occur to you, "Why am I defending myself? Why is it I've got to walk around defending myself all the time?" You'll get the idea, I positively guarantee you of that, Brother. It will occur to you. Of course. You really think that there is something outside of you that can harm you. That's absurd. It can't be true.

I teach further that because of your falsity of identification you projected from yourself images in cause and effect relationship and are literally being attacked by your effects. You won't hear that, but I assure you it's true.

Good morning.

Look at that — It's very phallic! Look at your own mind... You feel kind of guilty. You feel guilty, that is why you have to defend yourself. You feel guilty. Yes, it's what we term a primordial guilt that comes from leaving the garden. In the Christian aspect you really feel guilty. What did you do to deserve pain? You must have done something. You look around, "What did I do? I didn't do anything to deserve this." You didn't. But you think you did. Since you *think* you did you will inflict pain on yourself, because I assure you no one can inflict pain on you but you. Are you ready for that? "That is easy for you to say, but that hurt when I did..." Did that hurt? I knew that... See, I know that I am you so... Sure that hurt, why did you do that?

Coming at it in a little different way, we teach that there is a process that the human race, that you, as established, are going through to bring about the transformation of your perception; and in no other way will you arrive at the truth. Since there is no truth on earth it cannot be arrived at. You are literally seeking and attempt not to find. Because you are incapable of looking in and seeing that you are the cause of it to begin with. I teach that you are God — which is the fundamental *philosophia perennis;* which is the ancient wisdom — and if you are not, there is none. And that is as truthful as I can say it. You can turn down your face and attack me for saying it; you may choose to deny your own value, but you remember this: All evil is only limitation. Okay? You are only evil by self perception or an inability to see that you are all powerful. You establish yourself in limitation and then protect your parameters against outside forces that are not real. Okay? That's what you do.

I teach that in your innocence and surrender is your invulnerability. Do you mean to tell me that the poor in spirit find God? Who do you think do? Do you really think that you can participate in this illusion and win? All fundamental teachings will tell you to detach from it, that it is not real. It is your persistence in participating in it that keeps you here. Period! That is too simple. "You mean to tell me that if I decided that none of this is true I would not have to be here?" Yep! You'd be where you wanted to be. You have absolutely total power of all consciousness in the universe or there is no such thing as that, and since you are in consciousness it must be so.

If you want to present me with what no-thing is, I would like to see you do it. When you finally get your thing reduced down, you will end up with one thing and that is you. You can't get away from yourself. It is not possible. Okay? It is not possible. That's a good thing, huh? That is scary. Somehow everybody on earth thinks that they can keep a secret and hide from yourself. You can't. Who are you hiding from? Do you really think — okay? — that when you leave this room, that you walk out, that the same power of truth that is here isn't wherever you go? How do you hide? What are you hiding from? You don't know who you are, you are scared to death. You have a terrible underlying fear. What are you afraid of? "I don't know. I'm afraid of death." You are afraid of death. You want to take a look at that with me? It looks like this. Everywhere you look it's rotten. Everywhere you look around here everybody is in bodies and then they die and they put them down and they rot. No wonder you are afraid of death. Here you are walking around and here you are in this body and you are thinking you have absolutely no idea how you got here, where you are going or what is happening to you. Not only that, but no one on earth does.

No wonder you join the Theosophical Society, what the hell *is* this? I asked the Astronomers, they didn't know. I asked your religious leaders, they didn't know. I asked the Scientist, the Quantum Physicists, they didn't know. I asked my dad, I asked everybody and NOBODY KNOWS!!!

So everybody builds a certain group of parameters around themselves and dies. Is there such a thing as death? If you say so. But you remember this, you made it up. Period! This is a death planet. This level of consciousness automatically dies, because it is not real! Your perception of yourself is not true. Of course you die, because you've never lived. There is only one consciousness. And that is yours. Isn't that amazing? "Does that mean all of it ends and I can change it?" Yep. "So what do I do?" Quit participating in this. You do a little bit, but you won't do it all the way.

Yeah that. Don't participate in the world. There is no value in it. You are giving value to it. There is none. No value. Nothing. At what point are you going to value something here? At what point are you going to say to me, "I know that's true, but I have to make a living." Camel dung! There is no value here. If you judge it, you judge it falsely. That's scary, huh? No one accepts that. Yet I tell you it's true. And you are here because you refuse to accept it. And only for that reason.

You are here only because of self-identification. And that's okay, but why not be joyous about it? What is it that causes unhappiness? If you come to know that that is true and treat it gradually and go out and love and be happy. That's okay. I know people that have adjusted to death very well apparently. Everyone has to on earth eventually. Either you look at it or you don't look at it. Either you got Eros or Thanatos. Either you do everything you can to protect yourself from it, or you go out and play Libertine and say, "The hell with it, I'll enjoy myself." Either way you have acknowledged death and it's not true and you are not true. You do. You go into a cell and hide that and pray to God; you are still acknowledging death. You go out and live it up and do everything you are going to do, you're still saying… I say you can't. I say you are a good creator. I say you made all this up. Are you happy with what you made up outside of you here? Are you content with causing ten thousand people to starve to death last night? Does that make you feel good? Or are you going to not accept responsibility for it? That is the highest truth I can teach right now. I am at the crux of what you can't accept. But you will. Because you will come to know that it is true. You will literally change things by coming to know who you really are. That's a great truth. You cannot change it in any other fashion. You can't ban the bomb by carrying a placard. You know that, my friend. It's absolutely impossible. If you've admitted to the death, you've admitted to the fact.

"Let's all of us get together somehow and we'll protect our own self." You'll fail. Everything fails here. There is nothing else here.

You have one sole responsibility on earth and that's to bring about your own atonement, your own awakening through your own recognition. Through that process you save, you, literally, as a Christ, save the world from itself. That's what you do. It can't be done in any other fashion.

I'll get my Quantum Physics minister here. They don't like it. But they are at the point of total subjectivity. Is there freedom in that recognition? Total freedom. They are absolutely free to do anything they want to do. Will I pay the price for anything I do? Of course, you'll always pay the price. Why not, you've been participating, so what are your motivations for bringing about what you do not want? If you create things outside of you that come back to attack you, it's your guilt. You have attempted to defend yourself in some nature — we call that 'magic' don't we? We get all these energies and people go out and make magic, make things happen, like form and business deals. There is no such thing as exchange. Value cannot be given for value returned. If you think you can you are in duality. You failed and die. You have given value to something for which I will exchange with you. That's absurd. You already have it. There is nothing possible that you could have need of. You have separated yourself from someone else and presumed that there is a lack of truth or a lack of something. That is literally not true.

"I will give you these things and you give me back that, and then we'll both be happy." No, you won't. No, you won't. If you place value on anything — all right? — you can never reach your happiness. It's simply impossible. In relationship, let's you and I get together and make our love till death do us part, and we will share the mutuality of the pain and misery and death and work together on the relationship. How absurd. How absurd. "I'll do anything for you to help you. I'll go ninety percent of the way. I'll take out the garbage. Then will you do these things for me?" It will never work. It can't work. How then will it work? I will give you a clue. See? I am going to give you — watch me. You got it. You all got it. Very nice, did you get it all? Huh?

[singing] I am yours... One hundred percent!

Yes, isn't that nice? Thank you, you are extending to me. Oh Daphne. Oh, thank you, dear one.

See what we did? That's what love is. What did I do? I gave myself to you. One of the great discoveries you make in your awakening process is that you finally only give to yourself. I *am* you, dummy! If I give you everything, I win. If you take it in any fashion and attempt to hang onto it, *you* lose. Of course! What are you hanging on to?! You already *have* everything. Huh? You see? That can be practiced. I just did it. That's beautiful. Now we're both free, aren't we? Huh, isn't that astonishing? I love you totally and we're free. Love is not possession. Love is not hanging on, huh? Love is not mutual false identification. Love on earth is hate! You really think that you can love something and hate something else. That's ridiculous. What kind of love is that? To acknowledge that there is something that is superior and inferior to you is absurd, and it's impossible.

Hello. Good morning. Five in the morning I started, and I can tell you I am all through.

Lots of patterns here now. There are some nice patterns. We have some new elements here that will blend in. Communication finally is self-identification with yourself. And then you stand aside. All of those elements are in you. Hello, we have been waiting for you.

Questioner: Do their names signify anything?

When they came in they had names. Oh, you are talking about...

Q: The dwarfs...

That's Grumpy, that's…

Q: Do the names of the dwarfs…?

Well, there was Dopey, wasn't there?

Q: Yes

Okay, then you know! Sure, they signify whatever you want.

Here's Mary Jo or "Happy", as we used to call you… Yes, they signify everything. But you'll notice that Happy can be sad and that Dopey can be bright. And that Grumpy can be happy. And that Doc can be everything. He is the intellectual one. Hello, who said that? Isn't that amazing? They have all the qualities in them to be anything, right? Where do they work? They work in the mine, okay? They are working with the lead, making it gold. Very esoteric. Who is Snow White? She is you asleep. But you are not really dead, are you? The poisoned apple is in your throat. Okay, got it? Come on, of course. Will the prince come along and give you a kiss and wake you up? I guarantee you he will. Huh? Of course. And then all your seven energy patterns, you are all going to be [singing]: *Hi ho, hi ho, it's off to work we go*! Isn't it amazing? Everything that you do is a paradigm of what you don't want to acknowledge. It's impossible for you to do anything that is not symbolic of your awakening. That is an astonishing thing to discover, isn't it? You know it. Everywhere you look it's symbolic of this one single truth. Of course it is; what else would it be? Is there something separate from that single truth? Huh? I am conveying to you the highest level that it is possible to convey in the universe; I am attempting to convey it. It is not expressible in duality, so I am energizing you to the truth.

I have permission on this. It's a little bit like picking up a book — I am going to give you an intellectual analogy —

Kumar Swami. Beautiful. I mean he's got a lot of intellectual capacities in regard to the paradigms in art and literature, and he can really come to the truth. And one of the last things he said before he died as he arrested was, "If I had it to do over I would be more mystical than I was." As though somehow he was making the decision, intellectually, to do *this* rather than *that*. That's too bad. That is not true, literally. But you'll see it manifest in *Hillier*. They must do it, because if they don't — and this is just observation for you — you will get beautiful heads like Ken Wilbur — "transpersonal psychologist"... That's a misnomer; it's the opposite of transpersonal. He teaches personal philosophy. Isn't that amazing? Do you see what the earth does to things? They turn it upside down. It's not transpersonal, it's personal. He has the dilemma of being a transpersonal psychologist, so he teaches hierarchies and he recognizes that you can only see from the top down. Okay? Where he falls short is, it begins to reduce itself. Okay? He sees it become more and more subjective. And finally he ends up all down here; he ends up in total subjectivity, he ends up in existentialism, humanism. He knows it and it frustrates him and he doesn't know what to do. I don't know who is understanding this; it just came to me, but it is a great truth. The last art theory was total reductionist. It's like if I looked at you and said, "The transfiguration and resurrection are physical." Okay? And you'd say, "Yeah, I know that's true, I read it in the Bible." Not what I am saying. That's reductionism versus my total recognition that you must bring about the awakening within the channel of you. And it can't be done any other way.

Really what we are saying is, you can only do it through transformation. And you have the incredible dilemma that you can't transform yourself. If you could, you wouldn't be here. Because it is in your falsity of recognition that you are here in the first place. Now what the hell are you going to do? You can accept that intellectually from me. But what are you going to do? So you read somewhere that somebody got up to a beautiful temple and maybe you read Jakob Böhme and Meister Eckhart, and you have had these beautiful visions — oh, feel that — and the angels came down and there was a voice with incredible beauty… "Is that true?" "Yes, that's true." "Why don't you feel it?" "I don't know how to do that. I must not have the right karma. *They* can do that, but I can't." What's that? They argue. They argue. Don't separate yourself from that. They're you. It's your self-identification that's keeping you here.

These transformations going on with this group as identified in space/time are absolutely phenomenal. Your perceptions are changing. It has nothing at all to do with what you think. Although you will rationalize it at the beginning, or you will begin to see it is in fact happening to you. You'll go, "Oooohhh, I talked to the tree." Beautiful, what's wrong with that? Or, "Funny thing is, I saw this down the road and this one happened." Of course. "I healed somebody." Great! "I levitated." Wonderful. What about it? Where does that lead you? The reason of the simple truth. That you are in fact making it up. That you are divine, that you are God.

We'll go to Heaven together. We'll go to Heaven together. Is that all right? What's Heaven? What's Heaven, Theo? Is there such a place as Heaven? What's Heaven? Are we in Heaven now?

[singing] *Heaven can wait, this is paradise, just being here with you. And breathing the air you do, Heaven can wait.* Ooo, thank you, dear one That's very nice.

That's what Heaven is. Heaven is our surer truth. That's the sure and simple truth. If you will come to believe that I am the Christ you'll be in Heaven. Because I teach that you are the Christ. And it is your inability to recognize me as Christ keeping you here. And you are denying it up to the end. And after I am crucified you are still going to deny me at least three times. That's an astonishing thing.

Q: Chuck, what did Jesus mean when he told people to repent?

What did *I* mean?

Q: Okay, what did *you* mean when *you* told people...?

What did *you*? Say, *"I"*

Q: What did we mean when...

What did *I*...

Q: What did I mean?

That's closer. To repent means to return home, to give up the illusion, go and sin no more. If I heal you — and Jesus lays on hands and now you are healed — I say to you, go and sin no more, I mean go and no longer be separated from God. Sin is separation. The only sin that has arisen is separation. There is no other sin. Sin is only self-identification. Now, after self-identification — blechhh — everything turns to sin, doesn't it? Because everything then becomes sinful. You cannot be both. You are either totally pure or totally sinful. Isn't that amazing? You are either totally in Heaven or you are totally in hell, and that's your dilemma. This is hell. This is literally hell. That's what *re*pent is.

Dis-cover. We teach you mentally a process of returning; everything is returning to God. We are in a flow, universally, as expressed in Theosophy, of a return from manifestation, Mother Earth, female, back to the male flow. We are in a process of waking up, or returning, to essence light, okay? Universally in a rhythm of patterns there is a pure energy or flow, and it flows downward and breaks off into tribes or rays, like the seven centers

49

and the seven rays, or the twelve totalness in chromatic ability expressed in music or in art or in literature or color or mentally. Each of you is endowed symbiotically, or as an identified relationship, with energy patterns — I am not going to get into that. To the extent that we share those patterns — okay? — we can awaken love for each other for communication. Finally, up in here, it comes into focus. Heaven is right here, at the fifth level. Literally is Heaven where you and I know for sure there is a God. I come from Heaven to teach you this. If you'd care to look at it that way. Now, at this level the refraction has occurred that has brought about the rays, or various consciousnesses, where you will be pervasive in energy patterns. Like you'll write the music to something and I'll give you the lyrics. Got it? And you'll distribute it. And you'll sing it. But finally it's all the single truth. Okay? There is no difference in it. I may express that as talents to you if I choose, but I recognize perfectly well that I have all the talents of the universe in me.

You may express that. But it doesn't make any difference, if we are going to make beautiful music together let's make it. That's what Heaven is. Do you see that? The moment that you and I really decide there is a God, we are home. What would we do? There is no such thing as pain, there is no such thing as anger. See, everything automatically disappears, doesn't it? I assure you that's the way I feel and that's what I am. I guarantee it, that I am the way and the life. Through me you come. And you must say the same thing because it's not a problem for you. We are all Christ somewhere. That's why we teach this.

You have no need to defend yourself in any regard. You have no need to defend yourself. You are totally innocent, you are totally qualified to come to know this, I assure you. But you can't compare it to anything. And I know that's true.

You are here because you hedge your bet. You are afraid to bet everything on the eternal. What do you have to lose, you are going to die anyway?

Did you see what happened? See what happened when you did that?

"Aren't you going keep on marching to death with the rest of us? Don't you want to be on earth and go to death with all of us like we are doing? Don't you want to get cancer and die and share in pain and all the things that we do here?"

And you are saying, "No, I am not going to do that anymore. I don't think I'll do that."

"Well, you weirdo, what's wrong with you? Come on, get with us. Get with the rest of us."

At what point do you really allow yourself to see the truth? I teach in truth that the process is transformative and that you have no control over it, and if you'll let it go you'll flow to that truth. I teach in truth. I teach in truth that it's absolutely impossible to control it because the universe is not sequential. What you did yesterday has absolutely nothing to do with what you are doing tomorrow. Got it?! You are here because you think it does. You have established yourself insanely, separate from the universe and got into space/time. It ain't true. What happened to you? You wrote a script and they pounded it into you and said you did this and you became this and you had to do that. Now you're caught up in this terrible thing. And you remember what you did last week and you think you are going to have to do it tomorrow. You don't have to! Do anything you want. You are free.

Gently. You remember this — okay? — once you hear this with me. There is a lot of energy source here. I say this to you, enlightened ones: It occurs with the entire body. It doesn't occur by taking a little energy and pulling it down and mushing it around and getting parking spaces and all the other things that you use or whatever you use it for, to gain power or control. Whenever you do, it will always fail. All of you have a tremendous amount of energy. All of you have marched to a different drum from early on and all of you have known that this is not true and all of you are getting responses to that truth. That's why you are here. Okay? You can't fail. This has already happened. There is no way that I could be talking to you if it hadn't already happened. An idea never leaves its source. You have never left God. Yes, it's impossible for you to have left Him. It is impossible for me to express a thought that has not occurred. This is all confusion and chaos. You are getting ready to hatch. There is a hundred thousand billion births that you try to express and they have absolutely no meaning and purpose except that they'll hatch as you are hatching now. And then you'll simply, as that energy flows to that truth at this level, you will participate in the awakening process of yourself.

Could you see that? Do you see that? I know that you are me. I know it. It's not something that someone said, "We are all the same. We are all light." I have a perception that allows me to see that you are literally me. I know that I am talking to myself.

Got it? Now, there will be responses like, "Yes, that is true because the Christ is in you." The Christ is not in *me*. Who the hell am I, if the Christ is in me? *I* am the Christ.

Would I dis-establish from the Christ and be separate? Would I say, "I am I and the Christ is mmm." That's absurd! Anything that ever speaks of duality is false. And anything that ever speaks of death is false. If you go with that you'll really come along real good real quick, huh? There is only us and we're only one. And finally there only is one thing and you are it. Get that anywhere you want to, but accept it as true. The only possible evil there could be, or "adverse force" as you call it, is you. You're the ego, you're the devil, you're the monkey, you're the adverseful. Not anything else. Who the hell are you, if you've got God over here and the devil over here? That's absurd! It doesn't make any sense. No wonder you're in pain. Everybody thinks something outside of themselves is causing them trouble, not true. Not true. Accept responsibility for it and lay it at the altar. Come to the simple truth of *non*-responsibility and I'll teach you in truth, as Christ would teach you: You are responsible, as you identify yourself, for absolutely nothing on this earth. I mean literally NOTHING. It is your acceptance of responsibility for some things here that's keeping you here: Your judgment, your specialization. There is no such thing as special.

That's tough for the ego. Dammit, the ego wants to be different than something else. Not true. Now, the moment that you totally detach and say, "I am responsible for nothing here" that's death. And when you do that you will immediately perceive that you are responsible for everything, okay? I positively guarantee you I am responsible for everything on the earth. Not only am I responsible for everything on earth, I am responsible for everything in the universe. Try that. Boy, that's joyful! Do you know why? Because I know that I can't fail. If I am in a stage mentally where I am participating in this illusion — okay? — and my energies are dissipated, all I've got to do is lay any burden I've got down... Wooop, I am home! You literally cannot do anything that I would consider to be sinful, because you are perfect. If in any way you judge your brother as being different than you, you fail by definition. Of course. That seems too simple. But that's a high truth.

Very nice, teacher. Beautiful. I recognize myself there.

We all share a mutual secret. It's amazing, there is only one thing. You're perfect. Moment by moment, you can know you're perfect and then it'll slip away from you again. And suddenly you feel, "No, I am not." You can always tell when you are not feeling perfect about yourself, you judge somebody else. Got it? Everybody got that? The second you look outside you go, "That's beautiful; that's good; that's bad; I am going to do this; that's no good; I think that's up there." The moment that you do that, it's a judgment of self.

The moment that you're judging is all judgment. Gently, now, gently. One of the great beautiful things in your freedom is not having to judge. See, judgment is merely a form of limited perception.

"Where is she going? Oh, she is going to the bathroom. Well, I am going to have to do that." Well, the mind begins to... it's inevitable. I just saw you judge. Isn't that funny? It's very difficult to stand aside. Do you see what I am saying? Since you don't know who you are, you don't feel good about yourself, and you will always judge somebody outside of you. Inevitable. You can't fool me, because I know who you are. You think you can fool me, Son of God! Come on home. I know better than that. I know who you are. Come on.

I teach that persecution is impossible, that you don't know what you are. Neither did he when he went through that process, incidentally. There is a sentence in *A Course In Miracles* where he says, "I really didn't have to go through that." Another sentence in the *Course* says, "I know I wasn't real then." He knows literally that there is no such thing as Joshua of Nazareth any more than there is such a thing as you. He also knows that he *is* you, as I know that I am you. As I know we share the essence of the Father.

Q: Do you mean there is no Chuck of Naperville?

Nor ever has been. In space/time sense, he is not here. He was laid to rest. My God, let me tell you something about that. There was not one redeeming quality in that entity — NONE!

And after six days Jesus taketh Peter,
James, and John his brother,
and bringeth them up
into an high mountain apart,
And was transfigured before them:
and his face did shine as the sun,
and his raiment was white as the light.
And, behold, there appeared unto them
Moses and Elias talking with him.
Behold, a bright cloud overshadowed them:
and behold a voice out of the cloud, which said,
This is my beloved Son,
in whom I am well pleased; hear ye him.

A Stairway
To The Stars

How can you be free? What is freedom anyway? Is freedom to do what? Freedom to do whatever you want to do? Is that it? What do you want to do? Definition: total freedom is total absence of fear. Because total freedom is total love, or total extension of yourself in freedom, to include everything else. You see? You cannot be free if you fear, because if you fear you will defend yourself. How can you be free if you must defend?

If you are fearful you must believe that something can hurt you or attack you. If you believe that something can hurt you or attack you, you can't be free. You will have to build walls to defend yourself. We attempt to find freedom, say, in a dualistic society, in America, by stockpiling bombs, okay? Hopefully we can defend ourselves, and what? Remain free. It will never work. How could it work?

Countries, societies, can never be free until there is individual freedom, until you come to your own freedom.

There is no freedom on earth. There can't be. There can't be, because you defend yourself. You and I can get together and defend ourselves in apparent freedom, okay? We'll be free, we'll go up to the north woods and we'll get a beautiful cabin and we'll be by a stream; we'll go to Oregon and we'll be absolutely free and the hell with everybody else. That will work for a little while. Then what happens? Well, I don't know, somebody invades you and robs your cabin. You pick up a newspaper and they've dropped the big bomb and everything is futile anyway and you are dying.

By freedom, I mean eternal freedom: freedom forever, freedom from all disease, all pain, all hatred, all jealousy, all remorse. By freedom, I mean laying the burden down. Lay your burden down and be free. "Oh I don't think I'll do that, I am going to carry this around with me for a while yet, I need to do that."

Right above you is freedom. It waits for you. It just sits there and waits. You may have it any time you choose. The chains that bind you are your own, I assure you. Since you do not believe that they are your own, somehow you go outside yourself and think, "Well, now I can…, this is what is happening to me, this is why I am this way, this is causing this to me. If this changes, everything will be okay and I'll be free. That won't happen to me. I'll be okay." You forgot one thing. The reason that those things appear to be happening to you is that you are sharing in this illusion. Okay? You made it up. You made him up and you made me up. You made this up. You are dreaming. You are going to wake up, and you are going to discover that you made up the whole thing. You got your cause and effect mixed up. The things that are affecting you, are caused by you. You think that the cause is outside yourself. You made up a dream in your dream and it is attacking you. Isn't that astonishing? Those things are not real. Okay, this is the ancient wisdom revealed, are you listening to that? This isn't real. Okay? It is astonishing. That is not acceptable to you.

Really, the ancient wisdom is, since this is not real, you must be making it up. Okay? You make it up in a perspective of who you think you are. Since you don't know who you are, you make up illusions outside of you that are then projected back to you. When you come to know in consciousness who you really are, you will create yourself, or truth. Do you have it? Okay?

If there is in fact consciousness, there is only one consciousness. If there is only one consciousness in all the universe, and there is, okay, or there is not; and if there is not, then who speaks there is? Since there is only one consciousness and you are conscious, you must be all consciousness. If you are in fact all consciousness, if you perceive yourself as not being, that must be a false perception, and it is. Who are you then? Literally, you are all things, you are God, you are all consciousness. You must be, you cannot *not* be — impossible! You may separate yourself in an attempt to deny that, but the truth is that you are, and that is what you are going to come to know. That's all.

Know ye not that ye are Gods? That is the ancient wisdom. In your arrogance you refuse to accept your own divinity. Isn't that amazing? You feel non-entitled, you feel guilty. And you are divine; you are absolutely perfect. I assure you that you are absolutely perfect. Never mind the things that you have made up outside of yourself in defense of who you think you are. You can't fail, finally. What would you fail to?

The wages of your sin, or thinking you're who you are, can only be death, and that is the process that you will go through, isn't it? If you retain a false identity, you will die a false death, but since you believe in your identity, your death is very real, I assure you. Your pain is also very real, isn't it? Sure it is real. I don't stand before you and say you are an illusion. I can do that, but if you think you are real, the pain is real.

There is a certain point that will come to you as an entity where you say, "I am not going to do this anymore; there is more to it than that." Then you discover who you are and that is a process that you are going through now. It is very nice to know that you can go through that.

The only purpose that you have here on earth in this illusion, as identified in consciousness, is to overcome the process of self identification to go to total identification. Of course, that is why you are here. And that is occurring in you and will continue to occur in you until you complete the process.

Remember that you, as identified, can only be you; there is no separate identification. Those are facsimiles of personality; they are not real. But consciousness is real, finally, the only real thing. And since all consciousness is the same, your identification of self is the same as the self identification of the projections that you have made outside of you. The man being beaten with the whip is the man doing the whipping. I assure you that is true and that is this very single difficult thing to believe.

There is finally no retribution because there are no cause and effect quotients. Consciousness is not linear. Sometimes when you are extending from yourself, you project from yourself and cause pain to other people, you'll feel that pain almost immediately, if you have had that experience. As you raise energies in your body that will get closer and closer and finally you become, you become divine simply to keep yourself from being in pain. Divinity or coming to the truth that you are God has nothing to do with morality at all. It is not written on a template, on a tablet, it is contained in you. You will automatically become true because you recognize that you can only finally hurt yourself.

Will you be divine? Of course. You are divine. It is not self will that brings you to that. It is not enforced disciplines. It is the simple truth. You do it by extension of your consciousness and you can't fail.

So how can I be free then — finally? Freedom can only come by overcoming, or recognizing, the falsity of death. All fear is fear of annihilation, fear of the unknown. "I am afraid, now I'll have to protect myself, I don't know what is going to happen to me." So you start with that premise. The more you give up the earth, the more you win, the less fearful you will be. The more acceptance that occurs in you that there is a divine template, or template of perfection, that is bringing about this change in you, the more easy you will be and the more joyful and happy you will be. It is inevitable; you cannot not be that way. What are we really saying, what do we really teach? We teach finally that you have absolutely no control over anything. And that the more you let go, the more you detach, the more energy of truth will flow in you. That is all.

If this is not real, at what point will you stop defending it? The moment that you totally stop defending yourself, you will experience the resurrection. You will graduate in consciousness and you won't be here any more. You are here simply because of self identity. How many so called entities coming to transformation, or recognition, does it take to save the illusion of the world pain? One! Just you. That is why we teach only you can save the world.

Who can save the world? You. Since the world can only finally be your perception of it, obviously it cannot be saved outside of yourself. How could it? How could it?

61

You think that you can have things and hold onto them in your self identification. To have anything is impossible. You already are everything. Finally to have is to be. I am, therefore I have. If I can have something in lieu of you having it, that is absurd. How could that possibly be? Is there a scarcity of things? Are some things good and some things bad? At what point do you judge that? At what point are you saying, "I think I'll have this and I won't have that." What a terrible incredible burden is judgment. But what you go through in your mind to sort things out of what you think is good and bad or right and wrong is incredible. No wonder you get tired; your mind constantly has to sort things out. And when you get all done nothing stays the same anyway and you end up changing your mind about it. Astonishing!

You get all tired. Tiredness is a form of death; there is no such thing as tiredness, any more than there is such a thing as disease. You think so but, boy, if I were in a constant state of trying to judge something I would get awful tired too, trying to sort it out in your mind, no wonder you are tired.

Don't judge it. Stand aside from it. "Well then I don't have any opinions about anything." Well you don't. Don't have any opinions about anything. Don't participate in it. You don't have to. You don't have to do that. Really all I am teaching is that the choice is yours, and that finally you have no choice but to wake up and understand that this is not real. I don't know when you are going to do it, but there is no self identity anyway. I am very much aware, as I stand here with you, that you are not real in personality. I assure you I am aware that you are not real.

I don't think of you as Pat or Ed in any regard, or you; I don't. Why would I? Why would I think that somehow a facsimile of consciousness could occur that has things all sorted out? Would you be different from the other four billion entities established here on earth, and there are billions of stars? How would you be separate? How would you be different? How am I different from you finally? Not at all! I am you, I am you.

At the next level we will establish into brotherhood, or a recognition of a single truth. That is what we are doing now. We are taking the fracturedism of the essence of purity or energy as manifest in the various colors, the panorama of colors of energies that occur in us are variant in our own symbiotic relationships, so we combined them in essences of love or communication and recognition of identification of mutuality. That is what love is. You're walking along the street and all of a sudden you fall in love with a person that is walking, coming from the other direction, that is an identification of energy patterns that are the same in you. When you finally come to your own fruition, everywhere that you look you identify in love, because you see only yourself. Isn't that nice to know?

Everyone is you; you don't judge them in any other fashion. You want to be free? Love everybody. That is an astonishing truth. But how can you if you don't know who you are and you don't like yourself? So I stand before you and say you are perfect, you are forgiven, come on home, "Oh does it go like that, oh is that true?" Yes that is true; you are absolutely perfect, you can't fail. Then you extend from yourself the creativeness or the truth of your own union. That is all it is. There is some fear connected with doing that, because in self identification the death process is required for you to get into the flow of the next level of consciousness. And if you are coming up and looking at it and you are holding onto yourself, it is very painful. You try to self identify in the midst of a big spray of energy that is dictating a single truth to you and that can be very difficult.

When you go through the death process of leaving this — whatever you want to call this — "body", if you want to call it that, you will, and, as expressed, have periods of regenerative energy, or *re*collection, as described in the death process where the light is seen, the process of the karmas relived; but that is just the beginning of it, that is what you here now are undergoing in consciousness.

When you complete that, you will be awake without dying through the death process itself. That is what being born again is. That is what the process of union is. You yoga, you transcend finally and that is nice and you can do it. So do it.

"...they maintain their egos" — that is nonsense, there is no such thing as that. That means there is no God, there is no power in the whole universe by which you stand aside from it. Why would you define who you are? At what point do you retain identity and march to your own death? That's silly! Don't do it! All you have to do is give it up. You can't die. Now we are in the great hall together with the common truth we share. Now our energy patterns are very similar. We identify with a single light of truth, nothing will define that. There isn't anything to define it. What would define it? We stand in truth. All fear is gone. How could there be fear?

Big surge of energy just came up, look at that. See the colors? See that? That is very nice. Take your whole body as a relationship of energy, but don't identify with it; that is not who you are. You are not the body; that is absurd. Why would you be the body when you are in consciousness? What would be real about this? It is very beautiful. Everything is beautiful, all of it is beautiful. Is this more beautiful than this? No. Is it less beautiful? No. There is no such thing as more or less. There is only all. Astonishing!

I can't be more than you, but I can't be less. I am you. Amazing! You open up the door and there it is. Now, look at this. Oh, oh. That is lovely, that is all in you, very lovely, how lovely that is.

That's you. You are free. Just say, I'm not going to be an earthling any more, and, you don't have to be that. Earthlings are blind, deaf, and dumb — all of them. There is finally no such thing as little self. Do you see the truth of that?

Truth brings you to that wholeness of recognition of yourself. The you comes to itself in its totalness. Each time there is an awakening it is glorious and individual because it is the single truth. The truth that shares that with you is you. Well, that is beautiful to know that. It is you but it is more than you, it is all of the facets of you, the incredible beauty and loveliness and truth of you.

What would you fail to? What is there left here for you? What is there left finally in a school room when you graduate? You put away the toys, huh? What is left for you? Why would you choose to stay here? What is there here but pain and sorrow and death and loneliness and terror? Why would you choose to stay on earth? It doesn't make any sense. Go home. It is that simple. I remember you very well. You remember me perfectly well. How would we not remember each other? How can there be more than one total consciousness? There it is. Not only that, we're here. We are all over the place, everywhere. The vast energy that is assimilating into you is transformative. You have nothing to say about it; that is the joy in it. See, it finally happens despite everything you might think about it and try and do about it, and we share in that glory and love each other in it and come to union in it.

See, it is a beautiful process finally, because you are totally innocent. What else can you be? Or are you going to protect yourself, huh, or are you going to say "I know that is true but I better hang unto this..." Then, you let that go. You abandon, that is the fun, total abandonment is fun.

I will build a stairway to the stars for you, but you can't walk on it. I am making it out of light beings. You can climb that stair now. You can see paradise. How beautiful the lights are. Oh, look. Look Look there. How beautiful. Look. Very beautiful. Very nice.

Each time you come to this place and the change occurs, you are remembering again. It seems very familiar to you. You have been here before. Of course you have been here before. Do you remember now? "Oh, there, I remember, I remember all the light around it." You are the light. It's true. This is very familiar to you, you remember now. Your rays extend up to the light. You are part of that. It's an adventure. It will show you the way.

I have been there before, and so have you. It's all mind. It's incredible truth, it's deep within your memory that we danced together in the light.

That is lovely. How lovely. We share in the universal light. It is yours especially, it is yours. Hm?

You can't fail. You are already home. There is no failure. I am going to put on some music for a minute. You will be able to hear it.

[Music] Oh, how wonderful. Oh, that's nice. You can allow your spiritual awakening to be shared if you want to and that is very nice to me, because it is true. The harmonies that blend in, the responses that you have in your cells to this are extraordinary. The process goes on in you now. It is very nice to me that it is happening to you. You can't fail.

[Music] That's nice. You can give a little boost to that. It is real.

We will see you a little later.

Be real still for a moment. Oh, oh, oh, that is lovely. Why would you choose earth when you can have that?

You can't lose. The more you come to that, the more the light shines on you, okay, you come to truth. You can't fail. Impossible! You do it for yourself and you do it alone; it appears you are alone here and suddenly it opens up for you to see all the glory of what you are here for. It is very nice. If it were not so, I would not tell you that it were so, for you remember it very well.

In this manner, since we are talking about it now, at the omega point, about this. The illusion that's in the truth that is here is coming to us now. It is like a joke. Sometimes when you awaken and you look around and you see what is happening here and it is kind of funny, because it is so pitiful, you have to laugh at it. You have to laugh finally at what the entities do to themselves. It is not true, but they seem to do it. And each one of them has to go through that final individual atonement; it can't occur any other way. Each will have their dark night. Don't wallow around in it. They'll say, "Gee, this must be what is supposed to happen." That is what is supposed to happen. It has already all occurred, nothing new about it. Fabric of consciousness. It is not linear in any regard. What you did yesterday has absolutely nothing to do with what you are doing now, nothing, nothing. Nothing! Hear me? That is why you are here, because you remember yesterday. In fact, if you didn't remember yesterday it would be impossible for you to be here.

You had to establish yourself or you wouldn't be here. We are in the process of dis-establishing you. Did we come to smooth things over for you and make it okay in this hell? No, we didn't come here for that. If you want to get it smoothed over, you go somewhere else.

This is the truth. You want to carve your little heaven out of hell. You go ahead, you try it. This is the truth here. It is very joyous, because you are allowed to fail totally, so that you can win, so you don't have to hold on. You don't have to go through these motions of pretending everything is okay. It is not okay. It is horrendously, incredibly bad, it is awful. Don't tell me it is okay.

You can do something about it, and only you can do something about it, because you made it up in the first place. If you can't figure that out, just remember you have no control over it. Now that will make you feel good as you know well.

You don't have to hang on to anything. The only thing you could possibly hang on to or have is death. Nothing else, nothing but death do you hang on to here. The moment that you give it all up, you become eternal, period! Do you Hear me?

Subjective Thought

Everything is a reduction of a single state of consciousness. This is a fact. This is what, for example, all the quantum physicists and the biochemists and the philosophers are attempting to do — find an ultimate singularity or truth. It should be obvious to anyone in a state of real so-called analysis of consciousness to see that a "unified force field" is the same as God. There would ultimately be no difference in the idea of a unification of apparent objectivity to a singularity — that would obviously constitute God.

Remember that in this state of consciousness everything is reduced. Historically, in that sense, Paul reduces Jesus, doesn't he? Augustinian ideas reduce Neoplatoism. Of course. Inevitably. Newton, for example, is an offspring of Aristotle, who reduced Plato. Sure. Of course. Look right at it. There is finally no difference in the notion of Newtonian logic or Newtonian science than in, say, objective deification. They are the same thing. They're the same idea. Do you see that? The idea is that unity can be established outside of you. Obviously, then, the next step beyond that would be for science to establish what? First, the idea of relativity — which is an incredible exposé of consciousness. It's fun, historically, to look at how it occurred to Einstein, how it came about. The idea of relativity involved what could be termed a mystical experience. That's a nice thing to look at. And of course, it's true. It did.

Do you have an idea what the new, young, modern minds in two generations since Einstein really are capable of constructing in their own mind? Try to get a hold of this, if you can. You go and sit with a young group sometime, that's really in states of thinking, and we're only talking sixty, seventy, eighty years here. I'm just going to point out the obvious so-called evolution of the consciousness. This occurred with me in a very high nature. I remember very well. I was about twelve years old, maybe younger, and I suddenly was presented with a pop version of the notion of relativity. And I'll never forget the experience that I had when I looked at it. There was a deep intuition in me that caused a flourish of energy in my head, where I was automatically able to conceive of how completely rational the notion of relativity is. The problem that my mind subsequently had with that idea was to sort out the limited definitions that were applied in attempts to communicate to me what relativity was.

If you want to see a young mind work today, watch them take, for example, the negativism of Schopenhauer, shake it out in about two minutes and come up with the truth of it. Real easy. The young minds are doing that. They may do it in the nature of an expression of Star Wars or Darth Vader. But they do it in their mind. Can you get it? Do you see what I'm saying to you? They will take a beautiful, divine notion of Spinoza and refine it in a single sentence in *A Course In Miracles* and take it right up to its truth.

Do you see what happens with those minds? They are not reducing themselves to some sort of qualitative analysis of fractured-ism. They put together! And this is really what we're trying to bring about in your mind, do you see that? Can you see what we're trying to do?

Finally, the notion of Augustinian philosophy or Newtonian physics is highly regarded in a certain sagacity of limitation. For example, with the Pope who is a master of phenomenology, which is a high statement that there can be objective phenomena outside the single realization of selfness. The Pope will take it right straight up to the point of refusing to recognize that he is in fact instigating the phenomena. Do you see that? The whole basis of quantum thinking, of *A Course In Miracles*, of absolute thought without object, of subjectivity, is the notion of noumena, or that you are involved in any equation in regard to your thinking. Holy mackerel, how beautiful! We can teach that. But we must teach it through a process of recognition that the occurrence is, in fact, a form of exposé.

All limited consciousness is willing to acknowledge the occurrence of an expansion or realization, generally speaking, as to music, as to art, as to philosophy, as to science, as to religion. But the inevitable tendency reduces it to a form of duality, simply because the consciousness is not capable of a notion of what you might term non-objective existentialism. There is no truer statement in the Universe than *cogito ergo sum* — "I think therefore I am." But once you've arrived at that inevitable conclusion, the question continues to arise, "Ah, but who am I?" Whence comes this notion of my existence? Wow! What an occurrence. Yes!

Finally, it comes more down to the necessity for consciousness to verify itself. All that creation finally is, is unity verification or the extension of a total idea — how do you express that? This is in *A Course In Miracles*. Everybody finally only creates their own notion of themselves. Don't you see that? It falls into a limited framework of consciousness simply because they have identified themselves as separate from the single unity. Wow! What's more Newtonian than that idea? And what is more unifying than the idea of quantum, or the idea of a single force or congruity that finally has to arrive at the incredible delineation that the Universe is only consciousness? That's a simplistic thing, finally, because truth is extremely simple. It's the notion that truth has moving parts, or is somehow devious, that causes all of your concern. The requirement in coming to know that, involved in the actual process, is one of non-subtraction of the self in the relationship to everything that is apparently outside of it.

This is the process that we teach, which is nothing more than what we started out with in a conversation in *A Course In Miracles*, where we attempt to teach the consciousness to look at what is apparently objective, and not establish its reality, but rather ask it what it is. This disassociates you from your own memory patterns in association with duality — that's really what happens.

The problem that Brother Albert Einstein had with arriving at the conclusion of the unified force field, was only his inability to carry the concept of it to the inclusion of his own idea about it. He ended up with the inevitable apparent notion that God is rolling dice. And this is his expression. He said, "I can't believe that God rolls dice." Obviously, if there is such a thing as true objectivity, there is an element of chance that has to be involved. It would be inevitable, because there is no basic order in the concept of the apparent reality. Do you see? It causes futurizing automatically. It cannot not. Is that a little muddy, that thought? My mind is coming in too fast, I can't express it.

We may express it to you that it is impossible for you to have an original thought. You are thinking in the past tense, and any projection you do in the time/space sequencing must involve your previous connotations of yourself. You construct your future, in other words, based on your past — obviously — the consciousness, you, individually, the Universe.

Speaking to us now is Brother Andrew, who occasionally may appear to be some sort of antagonist, but in a very high sense presents Socratic ideas which are subsequently discussed in unlimited frameworks.

Brother Andrew: I have heard of a situation where a person was hypnotized, and given a suggestion that, at a signal, he would take off his shoe and put it on top of the fireplace mantle. When the signal was given, this occurred. When he was asked why he did it, he made up an excuse to explain the behavior which he didn't even understand himself. He said his foot was warm and he wanted to take his shoe off and he put it on the mantle because he wanted to make sure he knew where it was.

Whatever. We are looking at the idea that he had to justify the action. That's the whole dilemma.

Brother Andrew: My question pertains to behavior that you are attributing to us, that we may not be consciously responsible.

You are not, consciously. But ultimately, you are responsible for your behavior and do in fact justify it in some regard. This is the whole basis of what I teach.

Brother Andrew: But it's unconscious.

Who cares? You have forgotten God. What you can call the consciousness is limited to your idea about yourself and subsequently makes you stay within the framework. That's why I teach that it is indeed a transformative occurrence. You listen to what I'm saying. I am trying to change your mind-set in this regard. Obviously, every action must be justified or the action would not occur. The whole basis of what we teach is non-motivated action. Listen to me. I want to say this one other way for you. Obviously, the hypnotist was conveying to the other limited state of consciousness first a basic recognition of objectivity. The consciousness hypnotized did not say to the hypnotist, "What's a shoe?" I asked you to ask the hypnotist, "What's a shoe?" Do you see? Well, look at it. Obviously, the hypnotist and the one hypnotized shared a limited concept of the ability to take off a shoe, composed in some sort of relationship of energy that apparently constituted a body. All of it is objective thinking and limited.

All that you presented to me was limited. I can take it and move it up into a framework of truth for you. The justification of the necessity to remove the shoe is the justification of self-identity. It will inevitably occur within the state of consciousness. It cannot not.

Brother Andrew: How can we do the things that you're asking us to do when we don't even know the reasons why we're doing the things that we're doing?

Ah, but you have a perfect purpose. You have constructed an idea of unity in your head, and express it.

Brother Andrew: But I didn't do it consciously.

Of course not. Because consciously you deny it. You don't appear to, but in the state of limited consciousness, obviously, you are denying singularity. That's a fact. Now you may say to me, "I choose not to believe I am denying it." And I am perfectly willing to go along with the idea that you have not reached a metamorphic position in your so-called transformation, where you have access to a unified form of thinking. All I say to you then is, since you have constructed it in your mind, and you obviously have the capacity to bring it about, I would suggest that you do so. If you are determined to remain within a limited framework of your consciousness, we are now directly involved with what we teach, because the necessity for you to take off the shoe and put on the shoe is precisely why you're here, which is nothing more than a limited self- identification. What I say to you, in an attempt to stir you from this, is to inform you with certainty that there literally is nothing outside of your thoughts about it. If you were to look at it in that way, I would say to you everything that you think there is, is all that there is, and there is nothing but that. This will cause you deep concern because you are determined that there is a form of a discrete thinking that is occurring outside of your framework — which is exactly what Newtonian physics maintains. The quantumist has arrived at the incredible, obvious conclusion that there is no discernment between energies — that they're all finally the same thing.

The next and only final step that can be made, is that they are finally you. It does not matter how you constitute yourself, don't you see that? There is nothing to compare you with! You insist on comparing yourself with things that are apparently outside of you, as Jesus would teach in *A Course In Miracles*, and as it's taught by Buddha. Who taught it more emphatically than Buddha? Buddha is reduced automatically, Christ reduces to Christianity. Of course. Does Plato reduce to Aristotle? Of course. It goes on and on and on. Everything is always a reduction. But finally it reduces only to you!

Brother Andrew: How does Buddha exist?

In any attempt to define him, is an automatic reduction.

75

The idea of the next step, or the idea of the transformation occurrence, which occurred with Jesus Christ in the establishment of the capacity of the consciousness to evolve, which is what Christianity is, and all it is, was automatically reduced, and turned out to be a process of death to find life, which has no real reality. This is all in *A Course In Miracles*; in the text it's beautifully expressed. You finally do not die to live. You never die. It's your acknowledgment of the idea of limitation that's sustaining you in this state.

You are in a state of absolute objection to the idea of eternity, because it involves time for you. It cannot not involve time. If I say to you that you're going to sit there forever and ever, you refute me by standing up and walking and sitting in another chair. You understood me. Good! I see the way your mind is working. Your mind is working, obviously, only in the past tense. Everything that's constructed in you is based on what apparently has already occurred. If you do that, if you really look at it, you are not really thinking about now, you're only thinking about a moment ago. Obviously, you can't think about next week or next month. What is expressed in *A Course In Miracles* is that the mind of everyone on earth is actually blank. Look at it. So we attempt to bring you into the now, which is really what eternity is. Watch a human being come together in a group with an establishment in limitation and attempt to communicate. They will succeed only on a very limited level, but that is really all they ask for. They will say, "I don't require that you understand me totally, but it would certainly be nice if we would not nuke each other — that we would not kill each other, or that we could get together and have a little relationship here, or that we could certainly share a lot of common things until we have our demise, until we die."

So, in reality, there is absolutely no communication occurring here, except when it is transcendent. One of the high forms of communication is, if you go to the Chicago Symphony tonight and a thousand people sit in an auditorium and share an impulse of energy, a conglomeration of rhythms or patterns of sounds of the notions of the chromatic scale, they will enter in to a form of symbiosis of a very high nature. That's what communication is. Communication ultimately has nothing to do with the definition of it. If there is one thing that Jesus teaches in *A Course In Miracles*, it's that experience can be unified, or that God is experiential — that is the whole basis of the *Course* — and can be shared because we have an absolute common denominator of reality.

Let's take that one step further. It would be very nice if I could show you that, say I go like this, "Pffss blah!" It has absolutely no significance at all. Somewhere along the line you were determined in your mind, at that moment, to give me a cause and effect relationship in regard to what you considered me to be. It's absolutely inevitable. The basis of Zen, or a koan, I believe you call it, is to bring about a shift in your consciousness where you no longer are sequential in your thinking. Do you see that? And you go, "Wow, what's he's trying to do? Why are you doing that? Don't tell me you don't have a reason for doing that. You're manipulating me." At the very most you try to wake me up.

Brother Andrew: Your analogy to people sitting in the symphony and sharing transcendental consciousness is very a propos. But as soon as you go to open your mouth and talk about it, you've entered into the rabble, attempting to solve the problem at the level of the problem, and it can never be done that way.

Sure, I know. Agreed. Therefore, you're condemned to hell forever.

Brother Andrew: No.

Well, okay! Then as soon as you say no, you allow for my insinuation of energy into you in the sharing.

Brother Andrew: I allowed that. But as soon as you open your mouth, you are out of it.

Yeah, but I can't extend without energy. I can't extend without an idea.

Brother Andrew: That's how you generate your shakti.

Sure. Of course. That's the highest form you can do. That's what God does. You're right on the mark. God generates shakti by extension of a true idea, if you want to look at it that way. Certainly. But remember, only you can do it. The tendency is to think that somehow — Jesus calls it in *A Course In Miracles* an absolute relationship of brotherhood that is inevitable in consciousness — the idea of establishment in time implies that there can be one consciousness that has arrived at a particular point within the framework, that seems to be more advanced. I am absolutely, totally aware in my awakening that there are no degrees in consciousness, that there genuinely are not hierarchies of consciousness. The idea of a hierarchy or the establishment of planes of consciousness always occurs in the limited state as it attempts to identify singularity. And, in that process, it has a validity because there is obviously an application of the possibility of a revolution or an evolvement to a higher state, which is contained in the basic necessity to overcome. You can't do it any other way. That is not practiced at what seems to be a lower level. Obviously, a rhinoceros does not construct ideas of future and all that. Since you have done it in your own state, the total realization that that can come about in you is a very, very necessary element. There could be, for example, no ideas of what you would call quantum physics or relativity without the fundamental notion of Newtonianism. You have to have a concept of the possibility of objectivity. That's a form of evolution. Sure. And that all occurs within your own framework of thinking, if you care to look at it.

There are certain ideas involved in the incredible notion of non-discretion. There is a paradox that is contained in specialness — for me to convey to you the idea that you are totally unique and special — but not in regard to anything separate from you. The idea that you are unique and special is contained in all of your fundamental existentialism. It is absolutely inevitable. The only single thing that you can know is that "I am I." And we're back to that once again. Accepting the notion that it is transcendental, or theosophical, or gnostic, is a very major step.

Jesus will teach in the *Course* that all ideas of love are efforts to communicate. Finally, all communication is only self identity or an attempt to identify self. Limitedness can never convey. Jesus would teach that it projects rather than extends. It projects from it its concept of itself. This is what the fractured-ism is. The idea that is projected from the consciousness contains the whole, that is, it contains the idea of positive/negative or the idea of comparison or conception. What we attempt to do in *A Course In Miracles*, or in teaching a form of transformation, is to cause you to think without discretion, really, basically. That's what the atonement is. In the *Course* it is taught as: The limited state of consciousness in its attempts to perpetuate itself has established, in its own karma memory, patterns of resistance in order to sustain consciousness, or defiance or self-regulation. Limitation inevitably results in grievance or the idea that there is a form outside of you that could cause fear or attack or concern to you as a consciousness. The whole basis of your karma, of your memory in the schismed Universe of duality, is obviously based on self-subsistence in limitation. That isn't hard. Jesus in the *Course* says all of your thinking is what? Post schism. That is, you think in a manner that involves a continual breaking down in the limitation of your consciousness. Yes, it does, of course. But if you stop and look at it, there is contained in your fabric the idea of unity. Obviously, it is necessary that you participate in that equation.

Did you look at the chaos out there, as individual consciousnesses attempt to sustain their own identities? Wow! That's an amazing thing. No wonder it's chaotic. All of them are indeed unique in their historic patterns. There is not one single fingerprint that's the same as any other fingerprint. That's a nice way to look at it if you want to. And there's billions of them. And they keep breaking down and breaking down. Survival of the fittest, in reality, is simply survival of the limited state at that moment of its own individual consciousness. Limitation always divides. Wow! There are eight hundred and forty-six species of beetles within one square mile in the Brazilian jungle. Holy mackerel.

Brother Andrew: Are you saying we break down everything?

Yes. What you have done in your basic concept right there is broken yourself down from this table. You obviously consider this table to be separate from you, don't you? Why? What is that table? You're going to answer me by looking into your mind in a previous construction and informing me what that table is. If I keep asking you questions, you're screwed. There's no way you can tell me what that table is. You have absolutely no idea what it is in reality. Try it, if you want. These are just exercises. This is in the Workbook of *A Course In Miracles*. It is exactly what occurs. We can sit here forever; you never will be able to find it. You'll break it down, and you keep breaking it down, and you keep breaking it down. And you arrive at the molecules and then you will get into other divisions of it in your mind. Don't you see? Ultimately, what you do is give up and allow it to be a table and utilize it in your limited consciousness. This is what the fabric of society really is — the use of objectivity in limitation is all that we really do here. Then we'll battle each other over our ideas of what this table is. I'm very capable of killing you over my insistence that this is a particular table, or over the possession of the table, since it is outside of me and I want to hold onto it — the idea of scarcity is involved with that.

Brother Andrew: I can see it, but I can't tell you what I'm seeing. But I am experiencing that something is there. Does that mean I'm still off the mark?

You are off the mark automatically, but that's okay. Really what you have begun to do then is what? Examine your own projections or your own thoughts, which is a very necessary part of the awakening process. That's why I would teach you to look at the table and say, "What is it?" When you come into a framework of unifying in thinking, you may very well look at that table and see it as the Last Supper table, for example. You will see it as anything that you have constructed in your mind. The whole basic tenet of what we think, and you must get this, is: Conception always precedes perception. It is absolutely inevitable. Will you grant me that?

Brother Andrew: That means that I think of the table before I see it?

You must! You're sitting right on what I just talked about.

81

Brother Andrew: So I have the fear before the action?

You have the need to protect your own identity in your own framework of consciousness. Of course. You are only what you are. As you come out with that, as you begin to think, you construct all this variety and sustain your limited consciousness through variety rather than unity. It will never work. The dilemma of Adam having to name the animals is incredible. He ends up with a continual breakdown of species. Why? Because he's got himself separate from it. And he'll keep breaking it down and breaking it down. It's inevitable.

The way you finally teach it, however, would be simply the acceptance of your own thoughts. This is what we would teach in *A Course In Miracles*. If there is only your thought about something, in other words, if you are the conceptor of the Universe, you are a creator — I assure you this is true. Since you are in duality and self-protection, you have established and delineated in your own consciousness, relative states in ideas about what constitutes your makeup. We would teach it in *A Course In Miracles* that it is impossible for you to have a thought that will ever leave you. Here's the whole dilemma of guilt. If you are attempting to establish yourself in limitation, and obviously you succeed in doing it, you have by nature the necessity to order your thoughts. You cannot not do it. You automatically reject or sustain some thoughts apparently in your consciousness. This is in the New Testament, this is what Jesus tries to teach. In a very real sense — I am sorry — if you think of "murderer," you are the murderer. It's absolutely inevitable. You don't want to look at that. I know that you don't want to look at that. You do not want to be responsible for your own thinking. But you are. You will do everything but be responsible for it. Why?

Because you've constructed death. And you don't want to be responsible for death. Do you see? Can you see that one death is all deaths? If one thing dies, everything dies. Look at it. Death is limitation.

That's what we live in here. Death defines life. That means that you are basing your consciousness on the concept that there is an annihilation or a termination. Anywhere you look on earth, you have constructed a form of cyclicalness, or something that evolves. Really, it's an establishment of time and space that ultimately leads to an apparent termination. There are expressions that are not acceptable in *Course In Miracles* like: "Anything that is not forever is not real." Tell me something that is forever. You can't. Then you will attempt a concept of God. You will say to me, "God is eternal." But there can be no eternity outside your idea about it. What am I saying to you? God is your idea. Death is your idea. Look at it. Tell me about God. Tell me about truth. Tell me what truth is. You can't. You can only be it. The notion that you can have ideas is a very strange thing. Who are you, then? What do you have? You have ideas about things; you're simply separated. Can't you see that you are the idea?

Brother Andrew: Am I everything that I experience?

Yes. Only. Amen. You don't like that, though. You can't tell the difference between pleasure and pain, but you keep trying. There is a concept in the human mind of continuity, that we just spoke of, as a high necessity to the coming about of the realization of singularity. It occurs dramatically in the notion of reincarnation. The idea of a continuing consciousness has great validity. The problem with reincarnation is the sense of limitation involved in the obvious notions of separateness in the memory pattern. That is to say, you were nothing specific in the past, but everything in your own relationship of consciousness. I used to try to express that with the definition of the passion of the crucifixion where you were no more Peter than you were the Roman soldier. Everything is your idea about it. Now, if you have a mystical experience in reincarnation where you speak fluent Sanskrit... Of course! I have already allowed you that the configuration of your consciousness genetically not only contains all possibilities, but contains all previous occurrences in the whole schism. It is only your dream, brother.

History is not objective. History is not an occurrence of separate specific things. That is just in your mind that it is. What is history finally, except what you think it is, or what you arrive at in aggregate with your people at a particular time? We can arrive at a conclusion that Hitler was an evil man. And you'll get some people after fifty years to say he wasn't so bad. Isn't that funny? Everybody just keeps rewriting history. Don't you see that? History is always based on expedience of consciousness. For goodness sake! We'll rewrite it anytime you want to. What's nice to see occur in the consciousness is the taking of the allegory of duality, which is really nothing but what the process of awakening is, and having it reconstructed in your mind to a single truth. What is it you are trying to prove, when you ask these questions, but yourself in limitation? I'll accept anything that you say to me. It's time that your mind began to look at the occurrence of a fairy tale as having the reality of revelation contained within it. What's more mystical than the Battle of Waterloo? It's what you make it in your mind.

Freedom. Quite literally, what we ask you to do, say in the Workbook of *A Course In Miracles*, is to free yourself from your own limited configurations. As that begins to occur in you, it's an extremely joyous and happy and incredible occurrence because it is freedom. It begins basically with the fundamental idea that somewhere within the framework in which you are conceiving of yourself, there is contained a unity or a truth or a singularity. This is the tacit acknowledgment of duality. It is inevitable that the earth would not be here had it not somewhere, within a framework, however limited, constructed the conception of God or of truth or of wholeness. The next step that you will attempt to teach is that, since it cannot be found here, to gain the knowledge must be a form of transformation or a changing of the mind, or an enlightenment, or an "Ah-ha!" experience, or a resurrection, or a genius definition, or a symphony, or a beautiful poem, or anything that brings about a shift in your basic awareness of your relationship with what apparently is outside of you. This is the basis of everything that I teach.

We have reached, very nicely in this configuration, sociologically, the acknowledgment that gaining truth could in fact be transformative. It has always been known among esoteric circles. The whole idea of the ancient wisdom, the whole basic fundamental concept of the religion, Christianity, is based on knowledge of God being gained by a transformative occurrence or a resurrection. That is in all literature. It insinuates every possibility of the conception of man in duality. So if we are going to teach it, the ability that is inherent in the individual consciousness to conceive of itself as whole must be at least an intellectual presumption. If you come into a group, you must somehow assume, and do at some level, that you are there for what you might call a legitimate purpose: to come to know who you are. As I indicated, if you will look at this basket — this is really what's occurring in your minds now — and instead of saying, "You are a basket," you say, "What are you?" Don't tell it what it is. Ask it what it is. Do you see how simple that is? Obviously, if you tell it what it is, it simply becomes a configuration in your own state of memory or limited consciousness.

There is a very beautiful passage in one of the first twenty lessons in *A Course In Miracles* that reads something like this: I can get you to grant that the past is not now, so it's impossible for you to think about it in reality; and that the future is not now, and it's really impossible for you to construct it, so quite literally, moment by moment, on the planet earth, everybody's minds are literally blank. They are not thinking of anything! Do you see? All they do is construct the past as they have observed it, which is not now, and project it out into the future. It's a beautiful way to look at it. So we have people walking around, and nobody, quite literally, is really thinking at all. The upshot of that, or the actual reality of that, is that it is absolutely impossible for there to be any form of communication in the chaos. Why? Because everybody is simply basing what they see on their own individual concepts, on the past. It has no reality. Uh-oh! Now we are into what we really have to say about this. Quite obviously, if we have granted that there is a single source, you and I, individually and in consort with all other consciousnesses, must ultimately share that reality. And that's what we attempt to bring about in brotherhood. That's all.

The *Course In Miracles* calls it love. It has obviously nothing to do with love or attempts at communication that are fostered here in the duality, in the chaos. It couldn't. Why? Because love does not involve perception. Perception is always distinguishing. This would be taught in *A Course In Miracles* as: It is impossible for you to have a neutral thought. Try to. You can't. Do you see? It's impossible not to take sides in perception because perception or conception of limited self is based on taking sides, and subsequently you have the incredible dilemma of literally rejecting, or attempting to reject some of your own discernment.

High thought coming: An idea can never leave its source. Its reality is only contained in the whole, which is another way of saying that two things cannot know each other because two-ness is constructed on duality.

So you have the apparent species, Homo Sapiens, sitting in a state of duality in a virtual attempt to sort out his own fractured-ism, or his own consciousness, and choose in preference, things to sustain his limited consciousness. Jesus in the *Course* tries to express it this way: Everything around you is an effect of your thought and has no reality because your thought of it has no reality. One of the nice ways to come to know that is to at least acknowledge that if there is nothing outside of you, it can only be your thoughts that are affecting you. That's a nice way to look at it. Obviously, that's true. Only your idea about something, or how you have constructed it within your own memory or karma framework, gives it any apparent validity at all. Since the whole notion of limited consciousness is based on — again, *A Course In Miracles* calls it "attack" or "defense" — you might look at it in this way: a state of consciousness, where there is apparently outside of you something that could affect you without your acquiescence to it, is what causes all pain and grievance and murder and all the other things that go with it. Obviously, this is so. We can teach you, and you have come to learn, that you are being affected by your own ideas about things. That's very nice.

Finally, the Universe is only an idea. If the idea is limited, obviously it is not universal, so that the thinker cannot stand separate from the thought. As long as you believe in your limited state of consciousness, through constructed limitation, that the thinker can be separate from his thought, you will maintain space/time. You cannot not do it. The whole basis of the idea that you can stand outside of your own thought is what has created space. If I stand here in front of you in a limited state and say, "I am *Theodore Everybody*. That is a pole over there." I have obviously constructed what? A space between myself and the pole and the time that would be involved for me to move from this space to that space. If my idea about that pole is finally only a configuration in my own consciousness, it in fact has never left my thought about it. This is high truth. This can be practiced. This is what *A Course In Miracles* attempts to bring about in the Workbook in the first fifty lessons. In order to come to that, I may look at the pole and say to the pole, not, "You are a pole", but as the first lesson in the *Course* teaches, "I don't know what you are." What? Look what happened. I don't know what anything is. Wow! Look what happened. What's the next step? You look at the pole, and you say to the pole, "What are you?" What does this do, then, within your own framework of consciousness? This can really be practiced. It makes you, for that moment, come into the idea that you are extending a thought at that moment not based on your previous recognition of it. What did you begin to do? You began to think.

"Thinking" on earth has absolutely nothing to do with really thinking. This is all in the *Course In Miracles* in the first fifty lessons. That is a little disconcerting, and people who insist on grounding themselves to limited consciousness will look at me and say, "Well, that may be very true, but when my mind begins to do that, I become frightened because I am losing my identity. If this is not a lamp, I've got a very serious problem." Do you see? Yet I stand in front of you and say, "This is not a lamp." If I ask you to define it for me, you will look at it and proceed to break it up into parts in order to what? Authenticate yourself in pieces! It's amazing how your mind works.

Now this group is obviously coming into a high state of what you might call aggregate consciousness. What would brotherhood or communion be but the acknowledgment first of a singleness of truth, that is to say altruistically: truth is true and nothing else is true, which belies the possibility of relativity or actual separate relationships within a true framework of consciousness. That, then, can cause us to what? Flow within our own memory patterns! Remember that since limited consciousness is based in space/time on historic schism, it is necessary that you come to know that all of your thoughts in duality are, in fact, based on limitedness. Religiously that is called evilness, or the fall. What we are really doing with your mind is bringing you — because you contain what you might term the genetic capability to conceive of truth or God, (obviously, you can do it since you have done it) — to the realization that since everything is finally only your thought about it, you must literally be the truth or God. You cannot not be. It's another way of saying you can't stand separate from your own ideas. This is the whole basis of the attempt in space/time at Christhood or guru-ship, or the establishment of an apparent entity who has gone through a transformative occurrence and can convey, through energy or ideas or by whatever means, a form whereby you, individually in your consciousness, can come to know that truth.

Taught at its highest level in consummation, there must be an acknowledgment on the individual consciousness' part that it is, in fact, truth unto itself. That has always been taught. *A Course In Miracles* says emphatically that this is a course in knowing yourself. It couldn't possibly be anything else but that. And everybody nods their head. "Know thyself" is one of the fundamentals. But it's much deeper than that. You must know yourself, because there is literally nothing else that you could know. Wow! The presentation in the Workbook of the *Course In Miracles*, with the immediate inevitability of that realization, places everyone in a high state of denial before they even begin. You can't even open it up and you have a problem. If you start out with some of the basic things, they're nice to look at.

Lesson 8: The past is not here. When you think about the past or anticipate the future, your mind is actually blank. That's what I just said. Lesson 14: Let me see somebody gobble this one up. Are you ready? The world you see has nothing to do with reality. It is of your own making, and it does not exist. That's a nice place to start. It starts out very nicely. Everything you see is the result of your thoughts. No exceptions. No idle thoughts. A neutral thought is impossible. Listen. Lesson 19: Cause and effect are never separated.Thinking and its results are simultaneous. Holy mackerel. It is a fact that there are no private thoughts. Oh, come now. Somewhere along the line, I'm entitled to a little privacy here. Listen to me. You are entitled to total privacy, and in fact that is all that God has — total privacy. Can't you see that? You are all able to look very much at that. Since there is nothing outside of you, you are of course totally private. What is more personal than God? What have you done with your own ideas to cause something to be outside of you that could subsequently harm you or cause you concern or bring about friction in you? There is no reality in combat or friction. There couldn't be. It is not possible. Wow. You ought to begin to teach this: When you see separate things, you are not really seeing it at all. That's lovely. I'm throwing in Lesson 23 because nobody wants to really look at it. The only way out of fear is to give up attack and defense. Resist not evil. Do not participate in the chaos of your own limited projections. Wow!

I wrote some strange things down this morning. I did some song titles. This is a digression. *There's no assurance without occurrence.* That's a dandy. That is, if you don't undergo a process, you can never be sure of anything. That's the way you can always tell an awakening consciousness or one that's awake. You may not be able to know what he's sure about, but you can see that he's very sure about whatever it is that you're not sure that he's sure about! That's a lovely definition. This one's for you: *Try not to smile on your own denial.* That's a dandy. Somehow we admit that we're denying, and kind of take satisfaction in our own denial. Really that doesn't bring about anything. This one was designed for you, too. It's a definition of tantric yoga: *Finding lasting peace through a lasting piece.* Put that as a bumper sticker for tantric yoga people. Bless their hearts!

The acknowledgment that this transformation is going on in you can bring about an incredible serenity and peace because, as you refine your own fractured past through recollection of your own perfection, you allow everything that apparently is occurring outside of you to be as it is without attempting to ascertain its historic frame of reference, through detachment. Isn't that lovely to be able to do that? Each time that you do that, when you do not apply in consciousness specific cause and effect relationships, there occurs in your own energy relationship a pitching up or a raising of the energy. This is really what we attempt to teach is happening to you. Your mind will then begin to reconfigure incredible occurrences that have happened in your past associations. You will begin to see them in a new focus or a new frame of reference where they come together finally in an incredible single acknowledgment that the whole purpose of your state of consciousness was the metamorphosis that is now occurring in you. Is that beautiful?!! You then may want to study it in books, like you may want to quickly get a comparison between the I Ching and the genetic code. You may find a thrill in seeing that the helix in the genetic code is the same as the symbol of the I Ching, or the total potential of the Universe. You go, "Oh, my!" Then, as the shift continues to occur in you, you look about and you'll see in your mind incredible connections of color and sound and thought. Art and poetry and literature will all come together in a singleness of the very, very obvious incredible consciousness allegory of space/time. It's lovely. You'll take all of the fairy tales and translate them, not through a process of intellectualizing them, but rather a high form of iconism or symbolism, into the reality that they are to demonstrate to you the occurrence of your own transformation. You will find in this process that your mind begins then to what? Do it with everything. So when we look at this basket instead of saying, "You are a basket," or the next step, "What are you?" You look at the basket and say, "I know in truth that you represent me in truth, and by my realization of your wholeness I see myself as whole."

What do we finally teach you then to do? Reject everything you apparently think is real, in order to see that finally only you are reality. This is what we are trying to do now in this process.

As this occurrence reaches maturity in you, you may well experience what apparently is conflict. Remember, in your attempt to stand aside from your own limited ideas, you will be in denial and finally, defiance of the constructs of the earth. From a religious standpoint, each consciousness unto itself practices on an apparent moment-by-moment basis the denial of its own true self, and establishes in limitation outside of itself constructs in order to sustain, through memory, its own limitation. The real problem that you have individually in consciousness is that you have conceived of truth and harmony and love and God, and are not yet in a state to recognize that it is in fact you. Perhaps the way now for you to look at it is this: Everything is perfect unto itself because everything is only itself. There can be no consciousness outside of the total identity of a state of awareness or a beingness. The zebra does not suffer pain in regard to its own identity. It is constructed within its limited framework of memory to the configuration of its establishment in duality. Finally, since you have one percent within your genetic code that is at variance with a chimpanzee, you are not a chimpanzee. The chimpanzee knows perfectly well what it is. It does not construct death in its mind. It does not bury its dead with artifacts to sustain it in its journey in consciousness. The thought has not occurred to it. But it has occurred to you. This engenders then great fear in you, doesn't it? Because apparently obliviation is God.

Actually, what you do is construct a method of coming to God, or truth, through death. Wow, what a strange thing to do. As a Christ, as an awakening consciousness, you will come into this chaos and present the limited state with the inevitability of recognition that there is no death, there is no termination, there is no obliviation, and that consciousness, individually in its own consort of apparent reality, will always be in the state in which it finds itself at this moment. In actuality most consciousnesses are not afraid of death, for they have constructed it as an escape from life which they are indeed deadly afraid of. We have come to discover that eternity is not a long time, but only this moment when we share our truth in love and in joy and happiness.

We'll have just a little quiet time — when it's sleepy time outside. Be very gentle now. (Wow... He really had quiet times that were quiet!) That's very lovely.

93

You think with the Mind of God.
Therefore you share your thoughts with Him,
as He shares His with you.
They are the same thoughts,
because they are thought by the same Mind.
To share is to make alike, or to make one.
Nor do the thoughts you think with the Mind of
God leave your mind,
because thoughts do not leave their source.
Therefore, your thoughts
are in the Mind of God, as you are.
They are in your mind as well,
where He is.
As you are part of His Mind,
so are your thoughts part of His Mind.

The Miracle Is
Your Awakening

Here are a couple of talks that we gave in the fall of 1985 that speak from our heart and from the truth of us. We send them with all our love to our brothers on the West coast. Also to brother Ken W., to brother Tara. We know of what you are doing and bless you. Thank you.

We have a new brother, he comes to class. He reads *A Course In Miracles*. The words are on the printed page and to everyone who reads them, they convey or communicate a meaning that he has about himself. When he reads in consciousness the thought that appears, it is really initiating from his own consciousness. This is the whole basis of *A Course In Miracles*. In a very real sense, people who study *A Course In Miracles* are making up *A Course In Miracles*. They also make up the authorship, the delineation of where they want to add to it, subtract from it and configurate it in their own memory patterns. This is, paradoxically, exactly what *A Course In Miracles* says that you do.

A Course In Miracles is a mind-training endeavor to bring about a shift in your individual sense of reality. Period! We understand full well that when you read *A Course In Miracles*, you are unable (obviously because you are here and have the necessity to read it) to understand it. If I say to you there are no requirements that you understand it, but only that you become it, it is very difficult for you. Inevitably, the scribes or the interpreters of *A Course In Miracles* delineate it within their own limited framework of consciousness. They cannot do otherwise.

You may take all of the so-called ecumenical ideas that are contained in *A Course In Miracles* and prove to yourself and to perhaps the culture as a whole that there are a great many similarities between what *A Course In Miracles* says and what is ultimately said by all divine scripture or by all occult recognition or by all physiological or philosophical discernment. What about it? The limitation is your inability to think or conceive in a singular manner, so that you would recognize that anything that you look at, you transcribe to wholeness if you are conceiving it as whole. Example: this candle is either absolutely divine, perfect and contains the whole Universe or it is nothing. Your conception of the candle as separate from the basket is what is making you retain a sense of limitation.

Somebody says to you, "I don't want to study *A Course In Miracles* because it comes from the Christian historic vernacular." What the hell does that mean? All that means is that the individual in his own consciousness has constructed outside of him an idea about what Christianity is. It has no reality because there is finally nothing historically significant about explicit occurrences. They have no unity. If I say to him, "Well, what do you mean by that?" obviously what he has done is question the source. He has evolved in his own karma or consciousness a definition of what Christianity is. And obviously he is not correct; he is in a state of judgment in limited conception. If I say to you, "Well what do you mean by that?" He will say, "Well I'm making a comparison between Billy Graham, Pope John II, Joan of Arc, John of the Cross, the Crusades, Judas, esoteric Christianity in regard to New Jerusalem." What about it?! What is that going to get you if you have constructed an idea about Christ or about God in your own limited state? It is impossible to do.

The whole basis of *A Course In Miracles*, is to teach non-judgment. Inevitably, if you have constructed yourself in the past, you are in a state of judgment of your relationship with your own thoughts. As Jesus would teach it in the *Course*, you literally sort out thoughts in your own mind and project them out from you in order to ascertain the validity based on your own misconception of yourself. If I say to you, as Jesus would teach it in the *Course*, an idea never leaves its source — you are all ideas — what about them? How do you feel about your ideas today? As you look out around you, how do you feel about your constructs? Whose constructs in conception are they if they are not yours? This is the whole basis of *A Course In Miracles*. If you deem something to be outside of you that is beyond your control or was not perpetrated through a conscious thought or conception of yours, you are doomed to defend yourself from it, or to interpret it, or to consider it to be separate from you. And of course it is not.

The definition provided in all esoteric conglomerations of the awakening process teach non-judgment, will teach The Beatitudes, will teach The Sermon On The Mount (Matthew 5-7), will teach the first fifteen lessons of the Workbook of *A Course In Miracles*. The Master, awakened consciousness, Da Free John, teaches *A Course In Miracles*. Of course! There would be no possibility of you coming into an awakening posture in your own consciousness and not teach what I am saying to you. But remember, the process of coming to that is a process of expanding your state of consciousness or a literal transformative occurrence, and this is what's denied religiously and scientifically in the limited state.

Here, listen, I'm going to read you just one thing. This in Da John's new book, from the Dawn Horse Press. It is an ancient definition of what finally, or one of the definitions, of what an awakened Christ or an Avatar or a Master or an enlightened consciousness is. Very simply, "A Veera, a realized adept, a divine man, by affirming the essential worth of the forbidden, he causes the forbidden to lose its power to pollute, to degrade and to bind." That is an exact definition of forgiveness. He does not give the power of his own projections dominion over himself. He doesn't judge it. The process of coming to non-judgment is a transformative occurrence. If I sit here in front of you and through *A Course In Miracles* look at you and say, "You are a divine living Son of God and in consciousness the only living Son of God or the only manifestation of consciousness in the entire universe and perfect unto yourself," you cannot accept that from me. Yet I assure you that it is true.

You are not the sum of the ideas about yourself because the ideas about yourself are not true. Remember that you make history to conform to your own limitations. The history of man is not objective. It is subjective because history is only man's ideas about himself and it is rewritten constantly. To give a sense of objective validity to history doesn't really make any sense. All you are doing is verifying your own limited state of consciousness through the perpetration of an apparent memory or apparent past.

A Course In Miracles, the process of transformation, teaches you to become indiscriminate in the manner in

98

which you think. Is this a process? You bet your boots! What you have read up till this moment in *A Course In Miracles* and the manner in which you will read *A Course In Miracles* tonight will be entirely different. Remember that because of the nature of the consciousness that perpetrated *A Course In Miracles*, the insinuation of the energy, the whole of *A Course In Miracles* is contained in a great many individual aphorisms in the book. If you want to spend a whole evening thinking about one sentence in *A Course In Miracles*, rather than trying to assemble it in your own limitation, consider a single sentence like, "Communication must be unlimited in order to have meaning." Do you understand what I said? There is no communication going on on earth. Moment by moment, together we can have a moment of total communication, as we did just at that moment. We shared a common purpose. Think about that. Once more: "Communication must be unlimited in order to have meaning." Limited communication is always denial of love because love may best be defined as unlimited communication. If I dissect you in my consciousness or give you attributes or qualities in any regard in my limited conception of you, I have condemned you through my inability to realize my own wholeness. Holy Mackerel! How simple can I get! That's exactly what that sentence says.

Here's a beauty: Judgment is not an attribute of God. That's all you have got to know to wake up. Isn't that incredible, What I just said? Judgment is not an attribute of God. You say, "Oh, wait a minute. He judges whether I'm doing this or I'm doing that, this is coming or that's going or it's big or round or fat!" No! No! What would Truth judge? Untruth? How? How would there be untruth? Look at it. You take that sentence and think about that for the rest of the day. That will wake you right up. Why? You've got a total non-judgmental God but what does He require of you? Conformation to His thought! What is His thought? Your thought in Truth. How did you conceive of God without making Him real? By what method are you espousing to the possibility of a truth or a unity and subsequently denying it? Of course God doesn't judge.

In this particular section of the galaxy, a master computer was dropped off about sixty-five hundred years ago that expresses in total the unity and singleness of purpose of the universe. As the maturation of the specie known as Homo Sapiens, of man, matures, the energy flowed direct from this computer, which is totally unequivocating and uncompromising, to the inevitable occurrence of the transformation. That's another way to express it. Express it any way you want.

There are no idle thoughts. All thinking produces form at some level. Now you've got a bad problem. You really think that in privacy you can think about something that is not known to the entire Universe. You can't. Why? You are the entire Universe! There is no thought outside of you. If you are constructing this in your own consciousness, and I assure you that you are, how do you subtract some ideas or thoughts that you have from others? You can't do it. It is not possible. How simple it becomes for you, if you want to look at it that way, as Jesus would say to you, you are the savior of the earth and the only Son of God. Why would that be true, reasonably? Because you have constructed the earth in your consciousness. It has no reality except that you have defined it as real. I am letting you escape from it. Don't you see what I have given you? The power to what? To *re*-vision, to *re*-form, to *re*-cognize, to transform. It is not outside of you. It is you. I have given you what? Freedom! Do you want to take it or do you want to keep pretending that there's something that is going to affect you, neglecting to remember that you are the cause of this? This is the whole basis of what I know to be true. How simple it becomes.

How very provincial for you to acknowledge your own Christship if you are willing to assume responsibility for your own thought constructions. Inevitably, you deny a portion of you. Why? Because you are in a limited state of consciousness. It is impossible for you to order your thoughts or conceive of a yesterday or a tomorrow or a possible action without eventually feeling guilty about it. You cannot do it because you are in a state of rejection of something. You are making decisions as though somehow you can bring about an effect. You can't. All effect has already been perpetrated and is perpetrated by your individual thought at the moment you think it. How the heck are you going to teach this?

The basis of your dilemma in spiritual search is your inability to see that there could never be finally such a thing as potential. There is no such thing in consciousness or in the universe or in truth that is not now active but can be activated in the future. That's a strange notion. It appears to be that way and obviously I am teaching you in *A Course In Miracles*, that it is possible for you to activate your own karma potential, but I assure you that all the history of the schism is contained in a single flash, and that you continue to reconstruct it in your own mind. So if you choose to do that, you are in a constant state of denial of your own thoughts. This is in *A Course In Miracles*. The idea that the earth is here except in your memory is absurd. Obviously, the schism is your memory. You are dreaming. This is your dream. You fell asleep, remember? You fell asleep. Everything that has been constructed in the total state of consciousness is nothing but your own configuration in your dream. You have forgotten that you are the cause of this. How can this be taught to you? How can I teach an illusion? I can't. But I can show you that if I read to you a particular sentence, that you can look at it and as your frame of reference matures, through your individual transformation — physically, psychologically, mentally, emotionally — you will see in your apparent limited thought, a wholeness or a structure of wholeness.

Let's try another one. Some of these are very very difficult. You must choose between total freedom and total bondage for there are no alternatives but these. Which is a simple way of saying you are either bound totally and here forever, or you are in Heaven and you are free. There is no compromise. There is nothing in between. What a lovely thought. It is true just as you fear that to acknowledge Him is to deny all that you think you know but what you think you know was never true. All of you, individually, in your own consciousness, must come to know that the earth is not real. There is, and must be, a way that this can come about. But it is up to you.

The experiences and the change of mind that are going on in you and in the group of full endeavor are extraordinary. You are being made new on a moment-by-moment basis. It is a very lovely experience. Is it a process of subtracting the limited self? Of course. Is it a process of stilling the body brain? Yes. Transformative occurrence is not talking about the transformative occurrence. You cannot literally have an experience. You can only be an experience. My goodness! Definitions of experience, whether ecstatic or fearful, have no validity at all because they communicate nothing. They only communicate a limited idea or a separate objective observation of the occurrence, and always involve judgment.

It is a strange notion that Brother Sharon presented to Brother Glorious yesterday when she said, "Isn't it true that there are some real good addictions along with bad addictions?" as though somehow she could tell the difference. The whole dilemma of being on earth is obviously the discernment that some addictions would be better than others, when fundamentally, the addiction to self or to self consciousness or the judgment that there are degrees of an addiction are what hold you in bondage — the assertion of the self. It is a lovely notion. But I assure you, for everyone that you can find that will define one addiction as being bad and another good, I can present you with somebody who has what? Defined the most incredible addiction that you could conceive of and reject, as being simply divine. Do you see? It is obviously true. I knew a man that had the divine addiction of molesting three-year-olds. Is that more or less divine than someone who serves true purpose, who helps the poor? It has nothing at all to do with that. The expression of the selfness in regard to the addiction, or the satisfaction derived from it, is always limited. Who knows that better than an alcoholic, addicted to a pint of gin for breakfast? To say that he doesn't feel divine when he drinks, is absurd. Of course he feels divine. Does that make it a divine addiction? I suppose. How do you define bondage? Does that apparently free him? Is taking another special consciousness in bondage "until death do you part," a kind of freedom? How do you define that? It's silly.

Limitedness always binds. Obviously limitation could not occur without fear. Self-sustenance is always (and this is Lesson 76 in *A Course In Miracles* Workbook) the denial that you are under no laws but God's. You obviously have established an idea of the value of nutrition, of the value of maintaining an equilibrium in your state of consciousness. You do it and that is why you are here. If you open up the book right now and read out loud to me Lesson 76, you immediately go into a state of denial of it. It is inevitable. You are constituted on the denial of it. If you value it, you will not escape the consequences of it.

Wow! Cause and effect. Of course there is no action without subsequent action. Of course there is no thought without subsequent thought. The only way, finally, listen to me, to eliminate cause and effect is what? As we would teach it in *A Course In Miracles*, to see that cause is effect. There is absolutely in reality, no distance between cause and effect. That is why The Father is the Son. You can't have a thought that has not occurred. You may attempt to effectuate it later on, but the whole basis of what I teach you is to shorten your conceptual distance between what you think you do and the results that are forthcoming. I am shortening your time, brother. You think there is a time between now and when you die. There is not. You have conceived of death — you can only die now. If you do that, you will see you are eternal. If you put it off, you will construct a future based on your false past. It is inevitable.

Can I shorten time for you? As brother Jesus would say, we can shorten it immeasurably, which is the same thing as saying you can come into your now now and only now and transcend to eternity. Eternity is not a long time, brother — it is no time at all. What a weird idea! People say, "Who wants to be in eternity if it is like this?" It has nothing to do with it. You are fulfilled at this moment or you never will be. There is nothing outside of truth. Truth is true and nothing else is true. There are no degrees of truism. Truth is not relative. No wonder you are in pain and fear. No wonder. You think there is justice in limitation. You search for it. You "eye-for-an-eye" it! You set up quid pro quo — I give you this, you give me that back — all based on limitation. There isn't any such thing as that. You are everything or you are nothing.

How many times have I taught this? How many times have I said this? I have been saying this for ten thousand years. You stood on the Mount two thousand years ago and told me this, brother. You said to me, "Don't resist evil. Blessed are the poor in spirit. Blessed are the peacemakers. Blessed are those who hunger and thirst after righteousness. Blessed are those who are persecuted in my name. Your kingdom is not of this world. Know ye not ye must be born again." Wow! Again and again and again and finally what? I come into your sleeping state, into your dead state, and I tell you there is no death, that you are eternal in your own consciousness. Period! What am I making you look at? You can't escape from yourself. I am causing you, in your own consciousness, to go into a state of acceptance of yourself. You could never come to God by denial of yourself or your brother who is you. Period! Denial is always hate. Acceptance and forgiveness is always love. The incredible discovery you can only give to yourself is the biggest step that you could ever take in so-called conception. But your absolute recognition that you are the creator of this and that all creation finally is, is the giving of the certainty of your consciousness. If it is not refined, you will project it; if it is true, you will extend it because an idea in truth never leaves its source. That's how simple it is. Over and over again we say to you, "You are the universe. There is only one state of consciousness: it is you. There is nothing outside of you." This is the highest level at which any attempt at bringing about a transformation can be presented to you. And that's the occurrence that is going on. It is always up to you. You cannot lay or foster the blame or give the responsibility to your own projections, because you have already limited them by the definition of yourself.

Group consciousness will never find God. Group consciousness is false by definition. All consciousness is singular. We may get together in groups and attempt through therapy to bring about transformative occurrences. This is an extremely high reach in so-called psychology or transpersonal psychology, but finally each consciousness in his own configuration reaches the inevitable truth of himself and not through commiseration. Through recognition. Everybody hear me?

The total in reality is never shared. It is total only in you individually. Wow! What do we teach if it is not subjectivity, finally? Imagine that. That's a very fearful concept for you, brother. It is very difficult. You keep wanting to give honor and value to your own limitation. And you will do it by constructing family, you will do it by constructing self defensive mechanisms. You will do anything you can to keep from going through the process that will show you that you are in fact eternal and all consciousness. I have come to tell you that it is inevitable and that it will come about in you. And each moment that you make the choice to turn to it, you turn away from the falsity of your own projections. How simple.

Full commitment brings immediate result; so does infinite patience. Full commitment and infinite patience are the same thing. Prepare ye the way of the Lord. Lo I am with you always. I thought you said you went to prepare a way for me. The consciousness of the universe is here or it is nowhere. The incredible tendency to come here and then carry something different out with you — it is only you. That is what you are coming to know.

Wholeness is the state of consciousness. It finally has nothing to do with the coming about of it. The single development now coming into the earth is the always-present truth in this limited configuration that knowledge can be gained by a shift in consciousness or a transformative occurrence. This is very rudely denied, sociologically. Of course. There would be an implication that somehow someone would be more advanced in his ideas and be able to exercise, through ideas, control over his sociological situations. And in fact this is what occurs in the world. Of course. Everyone finally attempts to exercise control over their sociological situations. It is inevitable that they do that.

The notion that there is an involvement of genetics or karma in the response of the apparently limited consciousness or entity, causes the idea of varying degrees of maturation, which affords for all sorts of strange hierarchies, ranging from perhaps the Hindu system of the Brahmin to the untouchable or the king to the commoner, and includes all of man's ideas of himself in limited association with the final truth of his Godhood. For a Christ or an advanced so-called consciousness to come among you and teach that you may now undergo a transformative occurrence that will bring about a new consciousness in you, finally must be rigorously denied. The whole basis of your consciousness is on independence from source. There are many consciousnesses now coming into the New Age thinking where they are the cause of this. The direct quotes now emanating from all recent spiritual literature, and as far back as man has been here, indicate that your conception is what is giving this any form of reality it may seem to have to you. Of course that is very true, but what goes hand in hand with that (and here is the difficulty), in one sentence I say to you, you are responsible for this. You! And in the next sentence I say to you, you did not make yourself. Now you are caught. If you carry that a step further, what I said to you is, the earth is your construct, but the earth is no more real than you are in its actual communication or creative energy. We teach only come home to source.

It is a giant step indeed to get community, establishment, in this limited phase of consciousness, to even acknowledge that truth can be gained through an occurrence — through a transformative process, although it is taught everywhere in the religious community. The scientific community is inevitably faced with the dilemma of genius, as is art, and inevitably denies it. And more particularly denies their own obvious potential, since it is their observation of the art that was brought about through their own configuration.

The truth is that if you don't extend the idea of transformation, there is no possibility that you will ever communicate. It is the one single thing that you can say in the illusion: This can be overcome. This can be re-cognized. We can take your apparent diversity and bring it into singularity. We can show you a new way of looking at things. Perhaps we will show you that the most obvious occurrence here is the consciousness' realization that he has constructed death. And in the limited state in which you have conceived yourself, I assure you that you are going to die. But what a strange thing to do. Contained within you and your ideas, since you have expressed it, is an idea of truth and eternity. Why is it then that everything that you see here in limited perception obviously is in a state of dying? Cyclical — it keeps being born and maturing and dying. It is in a framework of time and space because you are in a framework of time and space.

Is there turmoil and pain, anger finally, in the idea of your ultimate and inevitable death? I would think there very well would be. Quite obviously all of your manifestations of disease, apparent hatred, attempts at communion, must be based on the idea of your ultimate death. That is absurd. That doesn't make any sense. But yet if I present you with the absolute proposition of eternity, because of the nature of your limited construction, you deny me and actively pursue retention of the limited consciousness that must inevitably lead you to demise or annihilation. How unreasonable of you. What would be reasonable about death? What is reasonable, really, about pain and limitation? Obviously, the basis of limited consciousness is recognition of a form of selfness, identified as existing in a state of limitedness or lack, with the obvious need to sustain that level of consciousness — to survive. If I present you with the proposition that nothing that is not forever is real, it requires your double take!

The notion that you have come into, that this is your construct, will lead you directly to the truth because it allows you to configurate the absoluteness that nothing is outside of you. Very simply, there is nothing without your conception of it. How paradoxical, the notion of objectivity or the notion of separation. It seems so absurd that anyone would look at the idea of two things being separate — obviously their construction then is based on not knowing, apparently, what the object is that they are viewing. That's crazy. That's senseless. So they study the limitation instead of the wholeness. They philosophize on their own false configuration — on their own apart-ness. Wow!

As you go through your regenerative process, you begin to stand aside from this chaos, and this can be perceived as very conflictual. You no longer feel needs to participate in sociological death rituals of relationships which reject, or the intense need to accomplish limited goals. These things lose their meaning to you. But since earth consciousness is only derived from memory, all of the entities in states of duality around you are constructing you in their own limited parameters of consciousness. If you deviate from that and they are unable to adjust to it, they will attack you or deny you. Of course! If you look at it from your own conception, it would be obvious to you that since you are the creator or miscreator of everything about you, the only thing that could ever cause you pain or fail you would be your own idea about it. Obviously, everybody here is going through anger and pain and attack and defense because of their own ideas. If we take the next step, we come to the inevitable conclusion that you are being attacked by your own thoughts, and of course, you are. You are only memory! You are a limited memory machine.

The direct necessity for the body in perception is based on the retention of memory, of schism, and it is all in you. It is not outside of you. Every idea that you are having and sorting out is still with you. You have an idea of beauty, but it is always in relationship with ugliness. So you shun, or put aside, apparently in your limited state, the ugliness. It does not go away. How do you exorcise ugliness or evil-ness, the devil, the limited part of you, the configurations of attack and defense? You can never overcome apparent evil by combating it. We stand on the Mount and say, "Resist not evil." Literally, do not defend yourself from your own ideas. The only thing that could ever be limiting or evil is your thought. Your kingdom is not of this world. You are not from here. All of your equations of apparent justice lead nowhere. All of your configurations of give and take, and have and hold, and live, and die, have no value whatever except the value that you have given them in your mind. You listen to me: if you give the earth value, it has value. You do not get rid of it by establishing its valuableness and then attempting to give it up. Of course! So we teach be whole and true and real and love and extend. Be defenseless. Mostly, we teach forgive. Never mind the equation that you are only forgiving your own thoughts. That will come next — that you can only give to yourself. That you can only finally forgive yourself — that will come next. We finally teach an occurrence of know yourself, that will come to you.

Dare you start with the premise that you are the only living Son of God? How else can you come to the truth if you don't start with the premise of truth? If no idea is outside of you, who then is true? Who is all consciousness in the universe? There is nothing separate from you. You hold the universe in the palm of your hand. How will the earth be saved then? How will we return to love and beauty and truth? When you change your own mind, and only in that manner.

Come, reason with me about the inevitability of your consciousness. Attempt within your own framework of memory and consciousness to conceive of death now. See how the veil comes over your head? Attempt to look at darkness. Attempt to see, attempt to conscious-ize annihilation. Do you see that the awakening process is the death process? The subtraction of the limited you is all that the transformation really is — the resurrection, the enlightenment.

The history of the universe is contained in you. There is no thought of variation in the construct of consciousness that is not contained in you. You are the I Ching, you are the master genetic code, you are all of history. Religiously: you are the way and the light. Scientifically: everything arises from your consciousness. If there is nothing outside of you, all apparent parts must contain the whole. I assure you they do. The whole could never be the sum of its parts if you are the sum-er. One plus one could never be two for the "plus" is only you. Wherever two or more are gathered I am there. Of course, how simple! Make the stew then, divine cooks, and when you finish jump into the pot. What an incredible idea of freedom ensues with the realization of the acceptance of the responsibility for the universe. The incredible knowledge that the universe is finally benign, that nothing ever really stands opposed to anything. Nothing is in friction with reality or truth. Wow! You lay down your rusty saber. You stand aside from the fray and you say, "I will not participate in this any longer."

How easy it is to see historically that the idea of Christhood must be persecuted, must be crucified. Of course. The whole basis of the configuration of consciousness in regard to establishment in limitation is based on the idea of death. If I come among you and say, "You cannot die," what I am really saying to you is that if you come with me, the earth will collapse. Of course. There is a beautiful quote from brother Jesus Christ in *A Course In Miracles* where He says you really think that you came here and found the earth in duality waiting for you to bring about its transformation. On the contrary, if you are not here in your own consciousness, the earth is not here either. That is why you are defined as the only living Son of God. There are no idle thoughts. Nothing in truth is discrete. What would it be discrete from? To what purpose would it stand aside from unity, or could? No! No!

All around you is energy, manifest in duality, broken up again and again and again. You look for reason in it. You look for it in the limited state of your own consciousness to bring about a unity. And that is your sole purpose in consciousness — to escape the chaos that you have created. Wow! To remember that you are the cause and not the effect. Wow! To realize that you are only Adam dreaming and will awaken at this moment to the truth of you. And all your yesterdays are gone. You can't construct your tomorrow. In giving up your yesterdays, you take all of your historic incidences and perfect them in the glory of the realization of their inevitable capacity to bring about your awakening. You do not stand in judgment of your karma, of your past experiences. You release your resentments. You forgive. You extend your love and you come home.

Is Heaven real? You bet your boots it's real! There is another beautiful quote of brother Jesus, where He says that nothing outside of Heaven is alive, which means that you are in a deep sleep with your death wish. The construction of death is fearful and hateful and denies truth. Anything that could die could never have been alive. Wow! Therefore be you grateful for the occurrence in you and be humble before the majesty of the universe. The truth will be made known unto you. You will recognize in your own self the fullness and wholeness of all consciousness. You will extend from you only the truth of you as you have *re*cognized yourself. Stand aside then. It is impossible for you to do a wrong. How difficult it is for you to accept absolute forgiveness. How strong the notion of cause and effect. How difficult the final concept that cause and effect stand as a single thing with no time between.

In our transformation teachings, we are shortening time, to bring you into the moment of your unity and of your truth. Is it experiential? It is only experiential. All around you are rays and energies and sounds of a creative universe. Your dilemma lies in the notion of potential. From the idea of potential, you create futurizing or time. All consciousness is full blown at all moments. Everything that could ever be, is running full tilt. Wow! Wow! And you are it! Don't bind yourself. Be free. Cast your bread upon the water. Is it a full endeavor? Does it require purpose? Yes. Full commitment brings immediate results. Of course.

You are individually very select. You are indeed chosen. Without you, Heaven could never be complete. We are at the omega point together. Therefore, be of good cheer. What does brother Jesus say in *A Course In Miracles?* Blasphemy can be defined as depression and anger and resentment. Wow! You can't blaspheme against God but you can against yourself, can't you? The truth has nothing to do with this. Only you have to do with this and in that acknowledgment is indeed your salvation. One and one are not then two. One and one are three; then one and one are one. What an extraordinary occurrence to see that Light, to know that it is really happening to you. That you are in this process. Not someone else. Not someone historic, not a guru, not a Jesus. The recognition that you, as a man, become Man-God. Just you! Wow! Teach that, brother. That brings the denial to the surface. It is a direct confrontation with the limited self. Is the ending foreseeable? Indeed it is. You have constructed it in your own consciousness and are bringing it about. Thank you. We thank you, dear brother, for the occurrence of you and your Christhood. Wow! We never could have done it without you. You are indispensable to the truth equation, and your creations await you in joy and harmony, and love and truth. Welcome home! Welcome home!

This is a most difficult thing. I've said this a lot of times, that this transfiguration, that this enlightenment, this transformative occurrence involves all of you. It is not limited to your body-brain, for goodness sake! It involves your ductless glands, if you will, but not in separation from the rest of you. It is totally involved. It would have to be. You cannot bring about a spiritual transformation without a bodily change. It can't be done. Of course not. The whole basis of the Apocalypse or the Revelation is the movement of the passion within your body, for crying out loud!! Is that too esoteric now? Wow!

The high prophet contained in the Edgar Cayce readings in the 1930's, the beautiful book on the comparison, the simile, the metaphor, the allegory of the consciousness of the body in relationship to the ductless glands and the churches in Revelation. Holy Mackerel! You are all history. That occurrence can bring about some very strange aberrations within your own state of configuration. Of course, and will! Finally, it requires acceptance of all of you. Everything that happens to you now is in direct correlation with your own transformative occurrence. It would have to be. Of course. It is going on in you. Yes, indeed it is! Wow!

All disease is a denial of spiritual energy or an inability to create in truth. Of course! If disease is real, there is no truth. You cannot construct disease or pain or sorrow outside of you and then repair it. It's a strange notion — the construction of an idol, a limited god, a caprice god. Wow! All power is given unto you in Heaven and earth. Greater things will you do than I have done. Where is Armageddon, then? Where is this incredible deliverance? Only in you! Yes! Very lovely! Thank you.

I want you to hear this. Finally, what is occurring in full endeavor, and this is in *A Course In Miracles* — this is a course in reasoning to the truth of mastership or Christhood or Avatarship. That is what we teach. The Master Da John, brother Franklin, incredible awakening consciousness, teaches the Eastern tradition with a lot of Western vernacular, the idea of his Christhood. He is awakened; he is the only living Son of God. Of course! We are just going to take that a step further, and he is much aware of this, and present you with the inevitable conclusion: since there is only one final state of consciousness in truth, that you must be that state. Now you can teach it out of *A Course In Miracles*. If you will look at brother Da John from the *Course In Miracles* or the Jesus idea, and forgive him totally, which is really all that we teach, you will recognize that indeed he is the only living Son of God. Who do you think is sitting around me here? Of course! The fault always lies in the judgment of someone somehow being what? Further advanced or further behind you in his spiritual acumen. But remember, if you judge him at all, you judge him falsely — and there, is the problem.

Inevitably, in coming to the truth, we create stages or hierarchies of consciousness, and this is in the sense of apparent reality, very true. But the second that a notion arises in you that you are in the fourth stage and identify yourself and are working on the fifth or the sixth or the seventh, that's absurd. The moment that you acknowledge the possibility of a seventh stage you literally entered that stage and denied it. You could not configurate the notion of God without being true. You are in a constant state, obviously of schism. There is a false notion in association with time that some particular identities or configurations are born with more capacities than others. That will keep you here a long time, brother. I am sorry but it is not true. You immediately, through recognizing another's apparent Christhood, have denied your own — unless you will recognize it fully, in which case you will see that you are only him.

Question: "Are you trying to say The Jews aren't the chosen people?"

We say that the definition of Jew is chosen, historically, and that all who have come into a configuration of apparent duality are chosen and have been chosen into truth establishment. It is inevitable. It doesn't have anything to do obviously with race or establishment on earth, but there is a big one-chromosome difference between a chimpanzee and a human being. You bet your boots! That is the chosen element. If ninety-nine percent genetically, chromosomally, of an ape is the same as a man, obviously, it is the other one percent that is the chosen part. But the dilemma is this: the chimpanzee is perfect in its chimpanzeeness. I have said this many times. You obviously are the only nutty one. You are the one that's in the denial of yourself. The only thing in the universe that doesn't know what it is, is a limited state of consciousness that has already acknowledged its wholeness. Wow, strange notion. It's a strange idea that you could be more than one thing. Never mind what it is.

The truth of you is always the truth of you. Not in variation but in singularity. Wow! I can't teach that. Wow! The universe is a sense of consciousness. It is a beingness. Obviously there is no necessity for truth to identify itself, that's silly — and it doesn't. Thank You. More later.

The Love of God is in everything He created,
for His Son is everywhere.
Look with peace upon your brothers,
and God will come rushing into your heart
in gratitude for your gift to Him.

Be My Valentine

L ife on earth is a compromise, a negotiation, an attempt to establish equanimity, reach an agreement where there is none. The latest form of love is the pre-nuptial agreement, drawn up by a lawyer, whereby everybody can still hang on to all their things, but they share some. What kind of relationship would you call it?

(From the audience) "A transaction?"

Yes. A transaction in a search for a particular result.

I want to look at Valentine's Day. So this will be a talk about love. In the last couple of days, I have heard a lot of expressions about what love is, what it isn't, and what it ought to be, and what it seems to be ranging all the way from "God is love" to "Love is a French Poodle." Both of which, incidentally, are true but limiting, in a sense, since God is undefinable and the poodle could only be defined in some sort of non-encompassing rationale as to a comparison of canus domesticus. "What was that? What did he say?"

We must finally love objectively: I love you for your ankles. I love your nose. I love your hair. I love your boobs. I love you for your intellect. I love you for your artistic achievements. I love you for the way you make me feel. I love you for your new boat. I love you because we go to the same church. I love you because you're black or blue or green. I love you because we share a lot of dislikes. I love you because somehow we are going to work through the dilemma of earth in our quest, and together we can find the answers. I love you because my father told me I had to. I love you in defiance of my culture. I love you for all the little things that we share together. I love you despite some particular idiosyncrasies you have, but I'll attempt to change them or just have to go along with them. Amazing, isn't it?

What the heck is love? One thing I'll tell you for sure, it's not a form of exchange. And if you start with that premise, it'll help you a lot. I've heard it said, and well-defined indeed, that love is finally giving. So perhaps before we define love, we should define giving. How many kinds of giving are there? There's the kind of giving I know in exchange, where someone who loves money pulls out a gun and says to you, "Give me your money or I will take your life." And you give him your money. And certainly you're giving it to him. There's the kind of giving that says, "We are required to give to Aunt Tilly a Christmas present in hopes that she will remember us in her will or exchange with us or give us a gift," or "What did she give us last year?" or "We didn't spend enough," or "We're not going to give her anything; she didn't give us anything." There's apparently a nice sort of giving where you, in the goodness of your heart, give something of high value to you — and then you are just a little disappointed when it's not properly appreciated or when the gift you receive in return does not seem commensurate with the value that you have placed on what you've given away. Then there's another level of giving where you give in absolute sacrifice. You take your life and put it on the altar of mankind and bathe the leper's wounds. You don't attempt to heal the incredible ache and sores that are in your own heart.

The kind of giving that we speak of that's associated and is in fact love, as defined within the nomenclatures we are expressing, is the giving with the absolute recognition of no need for recompense, where the mere idea that something would be returned for the extension of what you have given as a gift would be outside the framework of your consciousness. Indeed, as you transcend your limited identities, you will see that through the extension of you in gift, you receive the love that is a part of what you are.

One of the more difficult things to express to someone on the path is the idea of being a good receiver. You cannot be a good giver if you are not a good receiver. Feeling worthy enough finally to accept any gift that could be offered to you in love is part of the process that you're going through to discover who you really are.

Coming to realize that anything that is not forever cannot be given away is difficult. We are coming to understand, finally, that what we mean by love is creation. Love is only the extension, or projection, of what you think you are. How many times have you said in giving, "This will be a perfect gift for Uncle John. It looks like him." You have placed him in a particular category. You have identified him. Amazing!

The only thing that you can finally, absolutely, totally give away and still have is an idea. An idea is the only thing that the more you give it away, the more you have of it. But remember this, finally you can only be an idea about yourself. And the only thing you can possibly present to someone else as a gift is what you think you are or what you think they are, which is really exactly the same thing.

For what you think they are is only a reflection of what you think you are, isn't it? How much do you really, then, love the recipient of the gift that you are presenting them with? A lot of identities, because of insecurities, are able to love as long as they can keep something at a distance. We can then set up idols that are outside of us and endow them with characteristics or ideas that we admire. They'll fail us eventually, but that's all right. We can establish some other new fresh ones, then, that we can love. And finally reject.

I've heard it said, "I don't know what love is, but I know when I'm in it." Is love, then, an experience? Well, that's getting closer, isn't it? Yes, love is an experience. Creation is an experience. Creation, finally, is your gift from the Essence, from God, and your ability to be a good receiver. The only requirement that has ever been placed on you on this earth is to be able to receive in totalness your own heritage, or the gift of freedom and love that are yours.

"Oh, I know you love me a lot, but how much do you really love me? Will you be my Valentine?" "What do I have to do to be your Valentine? What are the requirements? How much exchange do I have to do?" The idea that in love absolutely nothing is asked in return is extremely difficult to come to in a dualistic consciousness because everything on earth is fundamentally, because of the illusion, based on reciprocity. You think in a sequential manner. You base everything you hope to obtain on what you have previously obtained. And then, it turns to dust. Then you look for something else. Then that goes away. And then you look for something else. You just keep looking. People walk around the earth and say, "All I want is just a little love. All I want is just a little recognition. All I want is just someone to share my life." Is that loneliness real? You bet it's real. When you find that love, is that love real? Holy mackerel, is it real! Why wouldn't it be real, Son of God?

Do you think that the essence of the feelings that you have inside you aren't real? Of course they're real.

Love is love. There isn't anyone in this room that somewhere in this consciousness hasn't felt love so intensely, they didn't know what to do. Have you ever been so much in love, you couldn't stand it? You didn't even want to be close to the object of your adoration. You wanted to just stand back and savor this incredible, ecstatic annihilation that was occurring to your system. You creep out at night so that you can walk by the house and look up at the light. That's a pitiful kind of love. Inevitably your hopes were dashed in some manner. You got up close and discovered that whatever you thought about her was not up to what you expected it to be. But the nature of that need is Godly. Of course. What else would it be?

Love, finally, in a very high form of love on earth, is expectation. There can be no final joy in fulfillment on earth. I am sure most of you are aware of that, because there is in you an innate dissatisfaction because of the need to complete your search or to find the truth of you. So love is sort of like the search for the other half of you, isn't it? There's only half of you. You keep looking for that other half, not knowing that that other half is in you. Will you be my Valentine? I expect you to be my Valentine absolutely and completely. "Well, I'm willing to be your Valentine up to a point."

That's what you say to God, isn't it? If God said to you, "Will you be my Valentine?" You would say, "Sure. What are your requirements?" He says, "Well, one of the requirements, you've got to be happy all the time. You've got to be joyous. You've got to be in ecstasy. You have to extend from you love and see only beauty. Can you do that?" And you say, "Well, who's asking me? How do I know you're really God? How do I know you can really give me those things?" God doesn't even hear you when you ask for something, does He? He already knows that you have everything. It's astonishing. "I can't give you anything but love, baby. That's the only thing I've plenty of, baby." It's amazing. It's a high truth. "Yeah, but do you really love me or are you just saying that?" Amazing, isn't it? That's the kind of love that will bring about your awakening. That's the kind of love all of you have found yourself in the middle of, only to have your ideas dashed to the ground because it didn't turn out to be the way you wanted it to be.

Sometimes it's difficult to understand that absolutely nothing on earth is finally going to turn out to be the way you want it to be, except death. And in the process of accepting death, you have limited yourself to the idea of pain, murder, greed and all the things that go with it on earth. "I want you to be my Valentine, but I don't want him down the street to know about it, and I don't want him to be my Valentine, just you." How early, as children, we are taught to subtract, aren't we? As part of our survival course, we are taught to distinguish and discriminate. When I was a boy we had hate Valentines. They came on little sheets, and they said awful, awful things. People sent them anonymously to other people. They'd say, "I hate you." Now the people we hate, we just don't bother to do anything. We hate them by subtracting them from our lives, from our ideas.

The problem finally, then, is being a good receiver, being able to say, "Okay, I'll take it." Because if I were to give you everything that you could ever ask for on this earth, it would never satisfy you. You know perfectly well it wouldn't, and that's why you're here. You have reached a stage in the maturation of your consciousnesses where you've looked down the line and seen that you're going to die. You've seen death, haven't you? You see that everything here dies. Wow!

"Well, if it's true that you have to give everything away, as Jesus teaches in *A Course In Miracles*, in order to keep it, what's going to happen to me if I believe that and I take all my stuff and give it away?" That's a good question. "That's easy for you to say. You tell me just to extend my love and give it away, but after all, I'm here on the earth. I have to eat. I have to have a house. I have to have a car. I have to subsist. I'm entitled to some things. I want to be able to send out Valentines, have people love me in return for my love. I have to do that, don't I?"

Coming to know the truth of you is a transformative process that has nothing to do with what you finally do in action on earth.

A motivation to do nothing will end up exactly in the same stew as a motivation to go out and attempt to do everything. There is no difference in it. You are on this earth and have constructed this earth because of a limited identification of selfness. As soon as you discover who you really are, the earth will no longer be here. Does that have anything to do with love? Yeah, it has everything to do with love. Because as long as you discriminate in your mind what constitutes beauty and love and desirability to you, you are rejecting other aspects or ideas that you have as less Godly or less true or less lovable. Because you reject these things from your consciousness, they do not disappear. They stay with you. And it is these things that you fear and defend yourself against.

If love is real, and I assure you that it is; if God is a fact, and I assure you that it is; if truth does not require your opinion about it to be true; and I assure you that it is, there could never be any such thing as evil or hate or lack or annihilation or divisiveness or manipulation or needs to identify or needs to perpetuate or needs to defend. "Are you saying, then, that love is only non-active? Is love agape?

Is love nothing but spirit? Is love something that I simply take myself up to some sort of mountain top and dwell in a kind of samadhi, sort of an ethereal neverland?" On the contrary, love is, love is — Amo. Love is totally active, with no objectivity. How do you express something like that? Love is the turmoil of consciousness in the act of being fulfilled. Love is the recognition of the apartness, of the loneliness, of the incredible longing, of the need fulfilling itself. Of course. Is it active? It's totally active! Do you think God's love for you is not finally a state of action? Of course, but not action in the idea of reciprocity, but action in the truth of Itself recognizing Itself. Is my love for you active? You bet your boots it's active. It's what? It's an extension of me. What is creation finally if it's not an identification of beauty, stemming from recognition of beauty of Self, or Source. Wow! What is it that we share together when we paint Valentines or listen to the music? We actively participate in the energies or the rays or the fabrics of consciousness. I'll say we do.

I've seen a lot of definitions of love as being objectively active, where the word love has the same connotation as fornicate, like, "Let me love you tonight. The heck with tomorrow." That's very active. And from that aspect, of course, amo requires an object, doesn't it? Then, again, I've seen it expressed in a very wishy-washy fashion, as we said before, where somebody just sits. It's a state of, "Don't come too close to me. I'm in a state of love. I love only Jesus, and the heck with everybody else." It's an astonishing idea. You want to see real objective love? Look at some exoteric Christianity sometime. "I love my guru, and I'll be unfaithful to him if I come to you." That's a strange idea. You listen to me carefully in regard to love and its objects.

Love is not finally beauty, although I've heard it defined as such. Beauty requires perception. Love requires no perception at all. As a matter of fact, with perception there cannot be true love because if there are degrees of comparison, there is an element of less-than-love involved, and God is never less-than. There is no second to love. I cannot choose to love something and reject something else. That's not love; that's hate. That's tough, isn't it?

You walk up to somebody on the street, and you say, "I love you." What's he going to say to you? "Well, what are you, some sort of nut? What do you want? Here's a dollar. Go get a cup of coffee. Why are you saying that to me? What do you mean, you love me?" Wow! I looked today at the earth, and saw the desperate attempts that the karma identifications, the personas, go through in attempts to communicate with each other. They are unaware of the absolute futility of it. They are unaware, then, that in truth the object — and this would hold with love — of their adoration, literally does not exist except in their own consciousness of it, and they have endowed it with characteristics that they will subsequently deny and reject. Brother Jesus in the *Course In Miracles* expresses it in this manner: He says you literally cannot see your brother, who is standing right next to you; and if you could for just one moment see him, you would see immediately that you share a brotherhood or a union in Christ and would be home together in your love. All you see finally is a facsimile of your own consciousness, of your own memories. You desperately want to love what's outside of you, but since you have literally, because of your association of limitation or guilt, projected the image out from you because you hated it and rejected it, you inevitably cannot accept the love of your own projections. Of course not. How could you? At best you can commiserate with them about death.

Sometimes, the path to find what we're talking about seems sort of rigorous and difficult. We read statements in the *Course*, and I teach in truth that you are afraid of the truth of you. If love attempts to come close to you in any true regard, you reject it and fend it off from you. What do you think love is if it's finally not Christ — if love is not finally man-God? You don't want anything to do with man-God. He would force you to relinquish the limited selfness of you. You're very much frightened of doing that. "Let's compromise together, and I'll overlook what I think you are, partially, and you overlook what you think I am, and maybe we can stay together until death do us part." And I stand in front of you and I say there's no such thing as apartness. You are never alone and literally cannot be alone. In the process of discovering that, you can have an awful lot of lonely moments, because if you didn't feel lonely, how would you ever know that there is such a thing as non-loneliness totally? The same thing could then be said about any experiences that you have ever had in all of your memory banks.

Everything that has ever occurred to you has indeed brought you to this point in time and space, where you are at this moment, hasn't it? Is there somewhere else that you would choose to be rather than here? Is there something better out there that you can love more than you love what you're with now? What is it you're looking for? What is it that you hope to find? You listen to me: You can't find it here; it's not here. There is no love on earth. Finally, when you come to experience in its totalness the feeling of the union that comes about through your transformative process, you will see immediately the falsity of the earth, and the unreality of everything that's around you.

I don't love you despite the things that I think about you. I love you because I know who you are. I don't love you because of qualities that I have given you, comparisons that I have made with you in regard to other personas that are apparently outside of you in this confusion. You are incomparable. Could the Son of God be compared with anything? What would you compare Him with but His Father, of which He is the same? It isn't that you think too much of yourself, finally; it's that you don't think enough of yourself. You limit yourself, don't you? You limit your capacity to love, through inability to accept the idea that contained in you is all of the essence of the consciousness in the universe.

Couldn't the universe love itself totally? What else does it do? Wow. Just look at what love really is. Because love apparently in the illusion of separateness appears to attempt to sustain itself, which indeed it does, does not make it less lovable. Does not God sustain Himself through you? I say to you in truth that there are finally no degrees in Godliness; that the state of beingness, the dharma, God's will is the unity and the singularity; that there is as much Godliness in this pencil as there is in anything in the universe. The universe is not the sum of its parts. Nor is my love for you the sum of adding up the various qualities that you have in order to arrive at the conclusion that you are desirable to me.

How nice it would be if you could finally figure out on the earth that everything would either be totally desirable to you or not desirable in any regard. You would then have eliminated all need to judge anything and would only love. Wow! We then finally give to each other the only Valentine that can ever really be given, and that's ourselves. As long as I hang on to any portion of my Valentine, I cannot love you completely, can I? So I give you love, and I ask nothing in return because there's nothing that you could give me in return, because it's only through the giving of my love to you that I may keep it and be loved.

How could I love if I just sat, separate from something, and allowed something to be outside of me? Indeed, love is active and it is creation. When you come to your final truth,

Son of God, you will discover that you are a creator. As I stand before you now, I am actually creating you, am I not? Do you not see that it is your conception that is bringing about your perception? Are you, then, creating something hateful? Are you making something that you don't like, that you want to get rid of? Strange. Jesus in the *Course* says nicely, protect anything that you value by giving it away. Wow! "Well, I tried that, and it didn't work. I went out and I gave a lot of things away. I wasn't appreciated for it. The world's simply no good, and there's nothing I can do about it, so I'll get along the best I can."

The process, finally, of totally giving, or giving of self, is a process of surrender or subtraction — or death is a nice word for it. I am bringing about in you a death process, and you'll still be here after its completion. Isn't that astonishing? Boy, that's a fun idea. There is no death, brother. If there were such a thing as death, how could there be love? Would you simply love something then until it dies? Then find something else to love, and struggle in turmoil. Wow.

Where do you find unity then? Where do you find this truth? In you. The universe finally is only your idea about it. How much do you finally love? What did you reject today as not desirable? How much did you protect yourself today from the projections, from your illusions? The quality of mercy is not strained. That's very nice. Sounds familiar. It's here all the time. Are you, then, a good receiver of the gifts? Be my Valentine. "I'm not going to give you a Valentine this year. I gave you one last year, and you didn't give me one back, and I'll always remember that." All of your grievances, everything that you're holding on to in the past tense; none of it is real. None of it!

For the first time, and I don't mean to think of time as sequential, but in this particular fabric or in this moment, we are attempting to teach the "illusion" (and perhaps that's a word we'll use in this regard). The Atonement or the changing of the mind or the resurrection is totally subjective, and depends absolutely on you to bring it about, and there's nothing outside of you that'll cause it. That's a very difficult idea for you, isn't it? The idea that you are responsible, finally, in your state of consciousness for bringing about peace and glory and heaven and the subtraction of pain, is very difficult for you. But you stop and think just for a moment. If you're in a state of consciousness — and I assure you you are because you say you are — I believe that you think you're you, but you can't tell me who you are, it is going to become more simple for you to accept the idea of maturation, that you are awakening from a dream, that you are coming back to an original origin. There's absolutely nothing new about this idea. It's as old as man and always occurs in revelation.

I'm going to express this to you: Any attempts I make to teach you what occurred to me in revelation are forms of corruption. I say to you that there are quotes in *A Course In Miracles* that are virtually identical to the great Pagan mystic Plotinus, neo-Platonism, or the Christian mystic Meister Eckhart, or more directly Meher Baba — Meher Baba has some quotes in *A Course In Miracles* — or me. It should finally begin to occur to you, on a direct intercession of consciousness that has occurred through scribeship from a different level of consciousness contained in *A Course In Miracles*, that there's one heck of a lot more to you than you have allowed up to this point. For goodness sake. That's what we're bringing about here. It's kind of difficult for you to understand that the only requirement there is, is that you come to your truth. There are no other requirements. Wake up! Wake up! Your creations await you. The tear in the fabric has been repaired. You're dreaming. This is all over.

It is difficult to feel love when you're being attacked by someone, isn't it? I just looked at the dilemma of consciousness where people who want to love are in villages where it seems like they're being constantly attacked and misunderstood. It requires a certain endeavor or determination. Faith maybe is the word. Trust. Make the commitment to Eternal Life or to the idea that there is no death. It is impossible for you to fail, so you be of good cheer.

Do you know something? As you get further and further along on this path, rejection won't bother you in the slightest. That's tough. It's very difficult to teach an initiate this, particularly when they get to a point where they're very sensitive, and they really want to love and they can't understand why they're rejected and why there's so much greed and corruption on earth. For me to say to them, "That's because that's the way that the world is", is difficult. They keep thinking that there must be something outside of themselves that will finally commiserate in totalness with the conclusion they have temporarily arrived at about themselves.

Finally, when you wake up, you will discover that you are absolutely, totally indifferent to what anybody on earth says. Why? Because you know it's not real. The intensity with which the identifications protect themselves is insane. Of course. I'm going to tell you something though. Once you discover the truth for yourself, and it doesn't make any difference to you, you will then begin to extend from you the truth of what you are. You discover that you are me. Who do you think is standing up here doing this? What do you think Brother Jesus finally means when He says in the *Course In Miracles* that God only

132

has one Son? No wonder I love you so much. No wonder I give you everything. Why wouldn't I? What would I hold onto? Nobody can give completely as long as they have a feeling of lack in them.

It's impossible for you to love anyone absolutely until you are love yourself. But you've all had your beautiful moments. The moonlight shining on the lake, the bark of a dog in the distance, the wind rustling through the pines, the pungent smell of mustard plant in the meadow; discovering just a tiny wildflower growing out of a crevice in a rock, a big swallowtail in the morning grass, the incredible feeling of lonely nostalgia when an ancient melody plays in your heart. What else would you finally be but divine? Those moments that you feel of completeness and ecstasy and serenity are part of your heritage. They are the real you. So it will be with you; so it is each moment that you allow it to be — not in preparations for tomorrow or next week or next year, a continuation of a limited idea about yourself, rather coming at this moment into what you really are, discovering through your surrender, through your non-defensiveness the invulnerability of the power that is you.

The species man has a covenant that has been fulfilled, and awaits your return to complete Heaven. That's the only requirement. Happy Valentine's Day! How good a receiver are you? How well can you finally see that it's the giving, and not the object. Sometimes it's a nice process when somebody does something thoughtful in their love for you — and I assure you that you're loved — you look very quickly at the thought that went into them doing that and how they went out and bought it, and thought about it, and planned to give it to you, and looked forward with the expectation of you wanting it. That's the beginning of it, isn't it? True receivers are always very humble because they understand that a giver finally gives through love. That's very lovely.

I accept your gift when you give it to me because I recognize you as the Son of God. I see you creating me in your gift to me. And in my acceptance of your love have I extended mine to you. And indeed there is no difference between giving and receiving, or ever could be.

"I give to you as you give to me, true love, true love." How beautiful are the words that come from the mind of man. Where else in the universe would words or ideas come from except from the mind of man? Are you mindful of your divinity today? Did you act as the Son of God today? I'm teaching a review at the end of the day. Run a quick tape of the day in your mind and say, "I didn't get it quite right this time, but hang on, am I forgiven?" And a big voice will say, "Oh, yeah, you're forgiven." Why don't you go out and make some big mistakes? I'll forgive you for those, too. But you remember this: You can't fool me. I am the truth, and I say that you can't fool me. I have no rationale. I will not finally reason with you. What would you hide from me? I know you. When you begin to do that, you'll have a feeling of cleanness about you. It isn't necessary that you go out and make reparations for things that you have done or imagined wrongs. Forgiveness is of the heart. Are you then afraid to go to the altar and reveal what you really think about yourself? Of course you're afraid. That's why you're here.

You take my hand. We'll go together. I'll take you right up there. When we get up to the last spot, I'll give you a shove and push you right through, and your dream will be over and you'll wake up Home. And you'll go, "Oh, I was dreaming." All of you have had intense dreams that seemed so real to you, and then suddenly you awaken and they are very vivid in your mind, "Oh, I was dreaming." That's what will happen to you when you discover the unreality of the earth. It'll be just like that. You'll go,

"Oh!" For many of you, that's occurring now. The more you come into that, the more it comes about. I'd like to have some quiet time.

Good morning. This is another day. It's actually two days after Valentine's Day, but Valentine's Day is every day that you allow it to be, isn't it, through your giving of your Valentine. Somebody said that they felt foolish, and that's what we're going to talk about just for a moment here, because when you're in love, you act in a very foolish manner, don't you. There's nothing finally practical about love. The moment that you make love practical, it's like trying to make God practical. There's absolutely nothing practical about God. How could there be? God is totally impractical. Everything that genius finally teaches, or master-recognition teaches, will always be foolish to natural man, and that includes love or the idea of total love. The idea of total love implies abandonment, or the giving up to the one that you adore — the extension of your total self to that so-called object or that so-called image or that perception.

There is no practicality; there's no rationale in God, finally. He's a burning fire within you that needs to be expressed. That's what you do, all day long. You walk around, attempting to express this joy, this incredible abundance that's in you. What is love, then? Well, we've looked at a lot of things that love isn't. Obviously, love is never a form of exchange in any regard, is it? Love is never objective; it cannot be. Love finally is never exclusive, and cannot be. So we have arrived at a lot of ideas about what love is not.

Now, what is love? Let's come a little closer to it. Love, obviously, is an experience. You agree with that. Would you then agree with me that God is an experience? Since we are in a fundamental agreement that God cannot be defined, that truth cannot be circumscribed, that love can only be experienced, shouldn't we then be about experiencing it? At what point have you, in these three days that have passed since the last talk, gone out and been very exclusive in your relationships? Remember that you suffer from a fatal disease called LP. That's Limited Perception. You are going to die because of it. I saw in the paper this morning that one of the Russian leaders is terminally ill. *Everyone* on earth is terminally ill. Did you think that? I mean, everybody on earth is obviously diseased. They have acknowledged, through their limited perception, the incredible, insane idea of termination. So obviously what's going to occur to them? They're going to be terminated. And with that termination will go their idea of love because their idea of love was limiting. And by limiting themselves, they have limited their innate ability to create, which is really all that love is.

Love is finally my total recognition that I'm making you up, and, by gosh, I better love you. To the direct extent I do not love you, I obviously could not love myself. The greatest admonition that a Christ can ever give is, "Love the Lord thy God with all they might and thy neighbor or thy friend or thy brother as thyself." Exoteric Christianity and being-born-again saviors to the contrary, you cannot love Christ without loving your brother, and the idea that you can is absurd. This is the whole basis of what we teach in *A Course In Miracles.* Of course it's much easier to love God from afar. It's easier to love, to respect, to idolize a guru in a white sheet sitting on the top of the mountain peak, and you can go and visit him, but you don't have to totally identify with him. With your brother you must totally identify. That's why until you find the Christ within you or in your brother, you can never find Him.

Is love, then, a search? Oh, yes! Ah. It's a delightful anticipation of fulfillment, isn't it? Sentences like "I am love." are very true. "The Father and I are one." "I am that I am." Of course. When you have experienced that moment — and all of you here have in moments of fulfillment — they are indelible in your consciousness as peak experiences. We teach in truth that when you transcend or change your mind or resurrect or are saved or are enlightened, you will live and extend from you a constant state of ecstasy — but ecstasy not defined as the opposite of pain, but only as truth or love. Did we get that? That's pretty much there. Which is much the same thing as saying, when you reach that state you will accept everything totally.

There's a point I want to make here. I understand very well that in your projections, when you look at something beautiful, you must judge it as more beautiful than something else. This is an inevitable process. Following your transcendence, what you experience is total self-love, or forgiveness of self, or non-guilt, which gives you a parameter by which you judge everything and love it subsequently. For example, if somebody said, "Do you see a poisonous viper as beautiful as a bouquet of roses?" they are speaking from a position where there is an implication that beauty is not finally a single thing. You remember this in consciousness: Everything is perfect unto itself except you. Can you hear that? You're the insane one. Do you think that that rose is not perfect unto itself? Do you think that that snake is not filled with total self love? Of course it is! Is the leaf on the tree not adorable to itself? Does a rock not churn with the molecules of identification of itself as granite? Of course it does! It knows perfectly well who it is, and it is fulfilling itself. You are the fault. You're the one that's schismed. You're the one that doesn't know who he is. Wow! Wow! You got that? Good. No wonder we teach: *To thine own self be true*, you dummies. If you can't figure that out, how could you ever go outside yourself and find it? You can't.

Now, the subtle difference that occurs in consciousness if you allow for hierarchies is this: The rock knows it is a rock, but it does not know that it is you. You may know that you are you and also the rock. For, indeed, if you are not the rock, you are nothing, because there is nothing outside of truth, which is totalness. Do you see? There is only a state of consciousness. There is nothing else. That's why you can only define yourself as "I am I." There is nothing outside of you. You are the rock. You are the plant. You are the sunset. You are the rich brown earth that we will harvest from. What else would you be but those things? And I don't mean that you feel like a tree. I mean that you are a tree. A little difference there. You know, people walk around and they will feel this energy come up into their throats and they'll glance and they'll see a large porker in a pig pen, and say, "Oh, I can feel that big sow rooting around in the mud. I feel just like it." And that's a great truth. Or you'll talk to the trees, and you feel as though they're talking back. And that's a very real thing. After your final transcendence you have no identity as being separate from the pig, so you can't possibly identify your pigness. Ha! Ha! Ha! I wish I could express this. Do you understand? You become the tree and the pig. That's really what love is, isn't it? Those of you who have experienced real union in mating, when you come together, you can't tell the difference in each other. Of course not. You mate! I'm not recommending that you necessarily mate with a pig! Excuse me! See, everybody immediately tries to go out and act within the limited frame of reference. No. No, no. Love does not have to do with what I'm speaking of; love has nothing to do with that. All that is, are attempts to sustain limited consciousness.

Love defined in limitation will always attempt, after self-identification, to perpetuate a degree of consciousness. That's what the survival of the fittest is; that's what cause and effect are, isn't it? When you overcome that, you will see that indeed you are love and nothing but that. That's pretty much our Valentine's Day talk of love. So how do you feel today? Lovable? Is it possible to feel unlovable for a moment and still be in grace? You bet your boots! In fact, feeling unlovable is exactly the same as feeling lovable. Can't teach that. We'll try. At a particular stage of perception, in order to feel lovable you must have a moment of "unlovability". Do you see? I feel totally lovable now, but just a moment ago I didn't feel lovable. When you become totally lovable, you can't distinguish between unlovableness and lovableness. Of course, because you can't judge it. That's how I know that I love you totally. I don't judge you at all. Wow! That's great highs. Get this, and you'll understand what we teach.

I cannot love you because of your qualities. In my own mind in schism, if I allow lovableness to be a quality, there's an obvious insinuation that there is something unlovable, and that's a fallacy. Everything is lovable. Finally, you come to know there are no degrees of love. When you come to know that, you'll remember everything. You'll return to your creative posture. Jesus in *A Course In Miracles*: Your creations await your return. How long have you been gone? Just a second. You were gone and you're back. You're not really gone. You haven't really left. You haven't really gone anywhere. This is Heaven. Where would you go? Where can you go

139

to find love? "I'll journey across the universe. I'll climb the highest mountain, go to the deepest valley in search of my true love." Everywhere you go, you are. If you stay here, you are everywhere.

I think finally we might say that love, like truth and God and completeness, cannot be described, but simply is. Sort of like when you're in it, you know you're in it. All we really teach finally is eternal love, because everything that is not eternal is not real. That's what we teach. Fear is death. If you believe you can die, you cannot love. You will simply commiserate. We are here to tell you that you cannot die and must finally be total love. That's all.

You listen to me carefully. We're adding another word to what love finally, really is: It's freedom.

All love on earth binds. Because of your limited state of consciousness, you look for protection in relationships of love and bind yourself to that because of fear. So what you really have is love/fear, or love/hate. If you want to measure your degree of love for someone who apparently is outside of yourself, judge the extent to which you release him. To what extent do you hold on to them because you think you can have love rather than be love? The highest truth that I can give to you is that you can have nothing because you are everything. You cannot finally have love because you are love.

If you want a so-called love relationship on earth to be absolutely successful and absolutely perfect and without deviation and without any elements that are untrue, all you need do is give yourself to it totally. Anything that ever could be lacking in what you construe as a love relationship is what you do not bring to that relationship. Period. Does that answer your questions about relationships, dear brother? That's why all love relationships on earth are compromises, aren't they? You don't know yourself, and they don't know themselves, so you get together and don't know yourselves together. How close is love to hate on earth? Right next to it. How close is love to fear on earth? Right next to it. How close is life to death? Right here, brother. Amen. Thank you.

All About
A Course In Miracles

To many of you now in this accelerated program of awakening, the continuing observation that not a single human being on earth really knows what it is, where it is, where it came from, or where it is going and nothing at all about itself in relationship to the universe that is apparently all around it, is becoming more and more intolerable.

———◆◆✕◆———

As a transformative imperative, *A Course in Miracles* will perfectly assist and accelerate the necessary confrontation of your objective self-identify and the whole subjective universe that surrounds you, so that you may undergo your inevitable experience of resurrection and enlightenment.

What you are afraid of, and deny through your own possessive fear, is your own illumination; your returning to God-mind or the memory of your transverse from temporal being to the reality of eternal life. So, it is your transition from death to life, from your old meaningless self-existence that is, in reality, long over and gone. It is a teaching of initiation or the determination of an individual mind to come to its own whole Universal Self.

It is the rite of your passage from time to eternity, from the apparent occurrence of separation to the remembrance that you are perfect as God created you. It is accomplished through a bright reassociation of your individual perceptual self-identity. It is an awakening. This unearthly catechism is directing you to the confrontation of the necessity of parting the veil. Every obstacle that peace must flow across is surmounted in the exact same way. The fear that raised it yields to the love beyond, and so the fear is gone.

DISCOURSES WITH
THE MASTER TEACHER OF A COURSE IN MIRACLES:
OTHER BOOKS IN PRINT

These are anthologies of transcripts of profoundly transformative talks given through the revelatory mind of the Master Teacher of A Course In Miracles. They are ideas about the means and method of the recognition of the transformation of our minds and bodies, as we freely escape together far beyond the Universe that is all about us.

Master Teacher's discourses always ignite intensely emotional responses in participants as they begin to undergo their individual mental reassociation and transfiguration. You may have highly charged enthusiastic responses to this wholly dedicated, totally simple, lovingly communicated message of truth. Indeed, this outpouring of freedom-to-create that occurs through the release of your former necessity to retain self-inflicted loneliness, pain, aging and death, is the bright contagion of whole mind.

These talks will act as a catalyst for you, the reader, in your own self identity of space/time, to undergo the experience of enlightenment necessary to fulfill your inevitable purpose for living: to remember you are whole and perfect as God created you.

The following titles are currently in print:
- ILLUMINATION
- HOW SIMPLE THE SOLUTION
- THE PARADOX OF ETERNAL LIFE
- TIMELESS VOICE OF RESURRECTED MIND
- GETHSEMANE TO GALILEE
- INTRODUCING A COURSE IN MIRACLES: *Scripture from Resurrected Man*
- LOVE: *The Sum and Substance of Our Eternal Reality*

FOR MORE INFORMATION VISIT: WWW.THEMASTERTEACHER.TV

Made in the USA
Charleston, SC
23 March 2011